CRYLUS

Plato

Cratylus

Translated,
with Introduction
& Notes, by

C. D. C. REEVE

Hackett Publishing Company, Inc.
Indianapolis/Cambridge

For further information, please address
Hackett Publishing Company, Inc.
P.O. Box 44937
Indianapolis, IN 46244-0937

www.hackettpublishing.com

Library of Congress Cataloging-in-Publication Data

Plato.
    [Cratylus. English]
    Cratylus / Plato ; translated, with introduction and notes by
C. D. C. Reeve.
        p.   cm.
    Includes bibliographical references and index.
    ISBN 0-87220-416-2 (pbk.). — ISBN 0-87220-417-0 (cloth)
    1. Language and languages—Philosophy.   I. Reeve, C. D. C.,
1948-   . II. Title.
    B367.A5R44   1999   98-37806
    184—dc21   CIP

ISBN-13: 978-0-87220-417-1 (cloth)
ISBN-13: 978-0-87220-416-4 (pbk.)

CONTENTS

For

Mark and Kate

PREFACE

Bernard Williams has described the *Cratylus* as "brilliant" and "tough-minded." I hope that a new translation (the first into English in seventy years), coupled with a detailed introduction, will increase recognition of the truth of his description and win new readers for this extraordinary work.

Rachel Barney, Myles Burnyeat, David Sedley, Paul Woodruff, and an anonymous reader provided helpful comments on earlier versions of the translation. John Cooper's careful and insightful responses to a succession of drafts improved every page. Bernard Williams generously read the Introduction and suggested, among other worthwhile things, the addition of §7. David Sedley commented on a subsequent version, saved me from numerous errors, and helped me to understand both his views and my own more fully. I thank all these scholars for allowing me the benefit of their enviable wisdom and knowledge. I also thank Teresa Robertson for proofreading the final typescript.

Everyone in philosophy has reason to be grateful to Hackett Publishing Company for its enlightened attitudes and fair practices. I have additional reason: Hackett has fostered my work for almost a decade and provided a level of support for it and for me that is truly extraordinary.

Preface to the Second Printing

I have taken the opportunity provided by a second printing to correct a number of errors both typographical and substantive. I am grateful to Robin Waterfield for drawing my attention to many of these, and to John Cooper for very useful suggestions on how to repair them.

INTRODUCTION

The *Cratylus* is about language, specifically about names (*onomata*)—a category that includes proper names, common nouns, adjectives, participles, and infinitives. On first reading it seems to be a somewhat arcane work almost half of which is devoted to a discussion of what appear to be far-fetched etymologies of Greek words. When properly understood, however, even this apparently unprepossessing material serves an important philosophical purpose. As Plato's most focused discussion of language, the *Cratylus* is essential reading for every student of his work. But anyone interested in Greek thought more generally, in the history of semantics, or in the philosophy of language will find that it repays close study.

The dialogue involves just three people: Hermogenes, Cratylus, and Socrates. Not much is known about Hermogenes. He was a constant companion of Socrates (Xenophon, *Memorabilia* I.2.48, IV.8.4) and was at his deathbed (*Phaedo* 59b7–8). Diogenes Laertius characterizes him as a Parmenidean (III.6), while the *Cratylus* itself makes it plain that he has often discussed names with Cratylus in the past (383a–384a). His views are sometimes represented as being rather silly. Such evidence as we have, however, suggests that he was, if not an original thinker in his own right, at least no stranger to philosophical discussion. It would be surprising, therefore, and on more than one ground, if his views were of no significance. For why would Plato bother to discuss insignificant views?

In one passage of the *Metaphysics*, Aristotle says that it was through Cratylus that Plato, "as a young man," became familiar with "the Heraclitean doctrines that all perceptible things are always flowing and that there is no knowledge of them" (987ᵃ32–4). In another, he tells us that Cratylus carried his Heracliteanism to extremes, and wound up thinking that "he could say nothing, but only moved his finger, faulting Heraclitus for saying that it is impossible to enter the same river twice; for he thought it could not be done even once" (1010ᵃ10–15). It has been conjectured that the moderate Heraclitean we meet in the

Cratylus, who thinks that language holds the key to being, was later transformed into the silent, hyper-Heraclitean skeptic about language because he came to believe that language and meaning too were subject to Heraclitean flux.[1] Whether or not this is true, it is a nice story.

Socrates is sufficiently well known that it is perhaps necessary to say only a few salient things about him here. If we distinguish, as many scholars do, the Socrates of Plato's early dialogues from the Socrates of the later ones, thinking that the former is more solidly based on the historical prototype, while the latter is increasingly a mouthpiece for Plato's own views, it is clearly the latter we meet in the *Cratylus*. The historical Socrates was exclusively interested in ethics; the Socrates of the *Cratylus* is interested in metaphysics, epistemology, and the philosophy of language. The historical Socrates did not "separate" the forms (see §4) from sensible, particular substances (*Metaphysics* 1086^b2-5); the Socrates of the *Cratylus* seems to make this separation (439b–440e), and draws on the theory of forms as something familiar (386d–391a; §4). When I speak of Socrates in what follows, therefore, it is the character to whom I am referring, not the historical prototype.

§1   Hermogenes and Cratylus on Names

Adam in the garden of Eden is giving names to the plants, animals, and everything else for the first time. If the names he gives lack all descriptive content (if they lack Fregean senses), he can hardly make a mistake. But what if they already have such content? Suppose Adam says of an unnamed boy "I name this boy Astyanax." Everything else being equal, that is his name, isn't it? But what if 'Astyanax' already means 'Lord-of-a-city'? Is it now the boy's name even if he is not lord of a city? Turning to a different example, if 'lion' means 'retractile-clawed quadruped of the species *Panthera leo*' and Adam confers it on cows, is 'lion' now a correct name for cows?

Hermogenes' succinct answer to these questions is this:

---

1. See D. J. Allan, "The Problem of Cratylus," *American Journal of Philology* 75 (1954), 271–87.

No one is able to persuade me that the correctness of names is determined by anything besides convention and agreement. I believe that any name you give a thing is its correct name. If you change its name and give it another, the new one is as correct as the old. For example, when we give names to our domestic slaves, the new ones are as correct as the old. No name belongs to a particular thing by nature, but only because of the rules and usage of those who establish the usage and call it by that name. (384c10–d8)

Thus, on his view, 'lions' is a correct name for cows, at least where Adam is concerned, and 'Astyanax' a correct name for the boy. If later on, Noah re-dubs a sheep and a pet terrier with these names, they become, for him at any rate, correct new names for these other things. The convention that applies to names is the one established by the name-giver. But there is nothing to stop another name-giver from appropriating the names of the first and establishing new conventions for their use.

The fact that Socrates raises the issue of whether the name-giver can be either a private individual or a community (384e) might seem particularly salient, but I doubt that Plato intends Socrates' query to carry such weight. The point he wishes us to see is simply this: Hermogenes grants authority over the correctness of names to the name-giver, whether he is an individual or a community, and to the convention for using names that he establishes in giving them. His authority does not itself have a further source in some other standard for the correctness of names. We take a similar view ourselves about many proper names. As Frank Zappa so vividly demonstrated when he named his daughter Moon Unit, one can give one's children whatever names one likes. Moreover, whatever our legal or official names are, we can introduce new ones that we prefer, such as nicknames or familiar names, and insist that others call us by them.

On Hermogenes' view, names, whether proper or common, and regardless of whatever descriptive content they may have, function for the purposes of reference as contentless *tags*. Their reference is entirely determined by the convention established by the person or community that dubs someone or something with them.

Hermogenes opposes his view about names to that of Cratylus. So what does Cratylus believe? We do not find out in any detail until much later in the dialogue. Right at the beginning, however, we learn that he thinks that Hermogenes' name is *not* 'Hermogenes', but that Socrates' name *is* 'Socrates', and that his own name *is* 'Cratylus'.[2] Yet, he quite clearly grasps the references of all these names, even the incorrect one. "Your name isn't 'Hermogenes'," he says, addressing precisely Hermogenes himself. Thus his view seems almost paradoxical: if it were true, would Cratylus be able to grasp what he shows himself able to grasp in stating it? Paradox aside, it seems that Cratylus' position lacks the ready intelligibility of Hermogenes'. It eventually becomes clear, however, that what Cratylus thinks is something like this: If 'Astyanax' means 'lord-of-a-city', it cannot name anyone who isn't a lord of a city (429c3–5). So if Adam gives it to someone who isn't a lord of a city, it isn't his name. 'Astyanax' is naturally fitted to someone who is a lord of a city and can't really be given to anyone who isn't (429c3–5). On Cratylus' view, then, names are *keys*. If they do not fit something, they aren't its name; if they do, they are. Hermogenes makes dubbing omnipotent; it always trumps fitting. Cratylus makes fitting omnipotent; it always trumps dubbing. Is either of them right? As Socrates says, we shall have to investigate the matter.

§2   Natures, Actions, and the Truth in Names

Though sometimes so puzzled that he has been "driven to take refuge" in Protagoras' relativistic view "that things are for each person as he believes them to be" (386c6–7), Hermogenes really

---

2. Both names derive from *'kratos'*, which means 'might', 'power', 'rule', 'sway', 'dominion', especially the kind of power that enables its possessor to triumph or gain victory. See P. Chantraine, *Dictionnaire Étymologique de la Langue Grecque* (Paris, 1990), s.v. *'kratos'*. It is somewhat ironic, therefore, that Cratylus should claim that both names are correct, since given his theory of the correctness of names, one might wonder how he could know that. If Socrates overpowers Cratylus in the argument, perhaps only he is correctly named.

doesn't believe it (386a5–7), and is quickly convinced that it has consequences he cannot accept (386b5–d2). He also rejects Euthydemus' hyper-relativistic view that all things have all properties at all times, because they are at all times as they might appear to a perceiver at some time (386d3–6). He thinks that we have absolute authority over names and their correctness, but that the natures of things have absolute authority over the correctness of our beliefs about them. It is this combination of views, conventionalism about names and realism about things, that proves untenable.

The Socratic argument that establishes this begins by showing that the positions of Protagoras and Euthydemus have disturbing consequences: if they are right, it isn't "possible for one person to be wise and another foolish" (386c2–4). But if that isn't possible, Protagoras and Euthydemus have somewhat undermined their own authority, since there is no reason to accept their views rather than those of anyone else. Besides, and this is the note that is more forcefully sounded by Socrates, their positions conflict with Hermogenes' securely-held beliefs, since he is convinced that some people are wise or good and others foolish or bad (386a8–c1).

Goodness and badness are the focus; they permit Socrates to show that high moral stakes may be at risk in the discussion of names. "Incorrect speaking is not only an error in itself, but actually does something bad to the soul" (*Phaedo* 115b5–7). But they are only the focus. For Hermogenes rejects the doctrines of Protagoras and Euthydemus quite generally. Socrates concludes that he must, then, be a realist where things are concerned:

> If it isn't the case that everything always has every attribute simultaneously or that each thing has a being or essence privately for each person, then it is clear that things have some fixed being or essence of their own. They are not in relation to us and are not made to fluctuate by how they appear to us. They are by themselves, in relation to their own being or essence, which is theirs by nature. (386d8–e4)

The conclusion is intelligible. But it might not seem to be irresistible, since it might not seem to have taken account of all the alternatives. Surely, Protagorean relativism, Euthydemean hyper-relativism, and full-blooded realism cannot exhaust the field. This is true. But it is of little real significance. Hermogenes is a conventionalist about *all* names and a realist about *all* things. If his position is shown to be untenable, this would be a powerful result, even if there are other options that Socrates leaves unexplored, such as physical realism combined with moral conventionalism.

Hermogenes agrees that if things have fixed natures that are independent of us, the same is surely true of *actions*, since actions "constitute some one class of the things that are" (386e6–8). It follows that if someone wants to cut something successfully, his action must accord with the nature of the kind of cut he wants to make, and he must perform it with the tool whose nature fits it to make a cut of that nature well. If he wants to prune grapevines, for example, he must use a pruning knife and cut just so (see *Republic* 352e–353a). If he tries to make the cut as he believes it should be made, and his beliefs are out of accord with the nature of things, he will not cut properly. But speaking or saying things is an action just like cutting, so what holds of cutting and other actions is also true of it. Hence someone will "succeed in speaking if he says things in the natural way to say them, in the natural way for them to be said, and with the natural tool for saying them" (387b11–c4).

We see the conclusion just around the corner. Why not rush to it? Names are the smallest parts of statements and are said or uttered when a statement is made. Indeed, saying things is just one way of using names. Hence if stating or saying things is an action, so is naming (387c6–d8). But if naming is an action, someone will succeed in doing it if and only if he names things in the natural way for them to be named and with the natural tool for naming them. True enough. But isn't it open to Hermogenes to agree to all this and hold on to his conventionalism, claiming that naming is done in the naturally correct way if it is done in accord with whatever conventions the name-giver happens to have adopted? If names are just conventional tags, isn't it their nature to be conventional tags? To prevent Hermogenes from replying in this way, we need to slow down and follow the longer route taken by Socrates, a route whose importance is now illuminated by the unavailability of the shortcut.

If we are to speak correctly, we must say things in the natural way. But what is the natural way? Socrates' answer has two parts. The first deals with whole statements. Something is stated in the natural way, if it is stated truly, and it is stated truly if it says "of the things that are that they are" (385b7). The second part extends this account to the names that are parts of statements. "Is a whole true statement true," he asks, "but not its parts?" "No," Hermogenes replies, "the parts are also true" (385c1–2). The natural correctness of names, therefore, like that of statements, is a matter of their truth.

Is this plausible? Consider the statement: "Astyanax is a man." If it is true, 'Astyanax' must *refer* to X, 'is a man' must *mean* 'is a member of the species *Homo sapiens*', and X must be a member of *Homo sapiens*. Hence the truth of the statement does not require that 'Astyanax' and 'is a man' be *true*, only that the first have a certain reference and the second a certain meaning. However, it is also possible to understand truth in a way that does make it applicable not just to statements or propositions but to their parts (or some of their parts) as well: a statement is *true of* the world if and only if the world is a certain way; 'is a man' is *true of* something if and only if it is a member of the species *Homo sapiens*; 'Astyanax' is *true of* someone if and only if he is a lord of a city.[3] Thus, the legitimacy of Socrates' move from the truth of statements to the truth of their parts may be suspect or it may not. It all depends on how he understands truth. Moreover, the correctness of his understanding can hardly be settled yet. It will depend on what follows, on what work he wants the conception to do for him. So, let's give Socrates his claim that the parts of true statements are also true and see what he does with it.

When a true statement is made, then, its constituent names are true; when a false statement is made, its constituent names are false. Hence, introducing truth has the same consequences for the action or activity of natural saying or stating as it does for the activity of natural naming. If things have natures, as Hermogenes concedes, and if truth is a matter of according with things, as he also concedes (385b7), a conventionalist account of

---

3. See Gail Fine, "Plato on Naming," *Philosophical Quarterly* 27 (1977), 294–296.

the natural correctness of names is ruled out. For a name is used in the naturally correct way when it is applied to the thing of which it is true, and it is true of a thing if it accords with its nature. The longer route has therefore paid dividends: a conventionalist account of the natural correctness of names is blocked.

When we use names, then, we say or imply that they are true of, and so articulate or "divide," the natures of the things to which they apply. Hence, Socrates concludes that names are tools that "divide things according to their natures" (388b10–11). We can now better understand this conclusion and see all of the various components that have helped to legitimate it.

But there is one thing we have omitted. Names are tools for dividing things according to their natures, but they are also tools we use to "instruct" (*didaskein*) one another (388b10–11). Why so? Why are names tools of instruction rather than tools of questioning or praying or cursing or expressing emotion or performing any other so-called speech act? Perhaps the answer is that 'instruct' is an overly narrow translation of '*didaskein*', and that Socrates has in mind something as broad as 'communicate' or 'convey information'. But it is more likely, as we shall see, that he is using the verb in its narrow sense precisely to underline the important fact that names owe their very significance, their very expressive capacity, to their natural correctness:

> We make names for all the other vowels and consonants, as you know, by uttering additional letters together with them. But as long as we include the force or power of the letter, we may correctly call it by that name, and it will express it for us. (393d7–e4)

The natural correctness of names, in turn, is a matter of their being true of the natures of things. Thus, in employing a name for any communicative purpose whatever, we are overtly or covertly using it to instruct, to teach or tell the truth about the world; for communication presupposes significance or expressivity, and these presuppose truth. Present-day philosophers make a similar point when they assign a fundamental semantic role to propositions or truth-bearers.

Another reason the use of names in instruction is important emerges forcefully in the discussion with Cratylus. Cratylus believes that the only way to discover the nature of things and to instruct others as to their natures is through investigating their names (435d–436a). If he is right, the investigation of names is first philosophy, being at once the foundation stone of metaphysics, epistemology, and via them of ethics. As we shall see, Socrates rejects this idea completely (§11).

§3 The Maker of Names

The discussion of tools which follows (388c–390e) begins with a familiar Platonic distinction between users and makers. Tools are correctly used only by those who have mastered the crafts to which those tools belong. A shuttle, for example, belongs to the craft of weaving and is correctly used by a weaver. However, the weaver doesn't make shuttles himself; that is done by a carpenter. Nonetheless, he does play a crucial role in shuttle manufacture. In the language of the *Republic*, he can tell the maker "which of his products performs well or badly in actual use" (601d9–10), and so knows "whether the appropriate form of shuttle is present in any given bit of wood" (390b1–2). By parity of reasoning, names are tools of instruction and are correctly used only by the instructor and those who use them as he does. The instructor uses names, then, and so is not (qua instructor, at any rate) a maker of them. Yet, like the weaver, he will play a crucial role in name manufacture. He will supervise the maker of names to ensure that the latter's products are fine ones (cf. 390c–d). It follows (though this is somewhat occluded by a bit of name-changing) that the instructor and user of names is the *dialectician*, who is first introduced under his true name, as the one who knows how to ask and answer questions, at 390c10–11 (see §13).

Hermogenes has granted that names are tools of instruction. Implicitly he has agreed that there is a craft of instruction, and that the instructor is its master. Thus far, one might say, near truisms are keeping him going. He does not know—at any rate, he does not have it clearly in mind—who or what an instructor is. Moreover, he does not know who the name-maker is or how we come to have his products (388d6–11). Thus, Socrates must prompt him (or jog his memory) for things to continue: "Don't you think that rules (*ho nomos*) provide us with them?"

(388d12–13). Hermogenes agrees somewhat hesitantly that he supposes they do. It is an unquiet moment in the drama. After all, *nomos* is at the very heart of his own account of the correctness of names. "No name," he says, "belongs to a particular thing by nature, but only because of the rules *[nomô(i)]* and usage of those who establish the usage and call it by that name" (384d6–8). Presumably, then, the expected answer here should have tripped confidently off his tongue. That it doesn't may seem to be little more than testimony to the unsettling effects of the Socratic elenchus that Hermogenes attests to later on (390e–391a). But the exchange is also important for another reason. Rules or conventions have now been given a role in Socrates' own emerging account of the correctness of names. Much later in the dialogue, when Cratylus is being cross-examined, Socrates himself explicitly acknowledges this (435c2–6; §10). What may seem surprising is that nothing is made of it, that Socrates does not explain just what role convention plays in the correctness of names. But, then, Socrates is Socrates, a fashioner of puzzles or *aporiai* to make us think for ourselves, not a conventional instructor or teacher, who threatens to stifle our own creative thought by dogmatically feeding us all the answers (§13).[4]

The rapid re-submergence of rules and conventions, once they have done their brief work of serving to identify the name-maker, also has another explanation of some significance. Once the name-maker is identified as "a rule-setter (*nomothetês*)" (388e1–2), "the kind of craftsman rarely found among human beings" (389a2–3), we naturally expect the subsequent account of name-making to consist largely of a discussion of how to establish rules. One reason that it doesn't, beyond the larger purposes of Socratic instruction just mentioned, is the pervasive influence of craft analogies on Plato's thought in general, and on the present argument with Hermogenes in particular. For rules are not the products of any of the familiar handicrafts; a carpenter makes shuttles, not rules. Hence, if the craft analogy is to continue to guide the discussion as Socrates wants it to (389a6), rules cannot at this point remain at center stage.

---

4. See my *Socrates in the Apology* (Indianapolis, 1989), §3.8.

§4 Natures and Forms, Names and Shuttles

Socrates' general account of the handicrafts introduces *forms* for the first time in the dialogue. "Where," Socrates asks, "does a carpenter look in making a shuttle? Isn't it to that sort of thing whose nature is to weave?" (389a6–8). A few lines later, as in a similar context in the *Republic* (596b6–9), this entity is identified as "the form (*eidos*)" of a shuttle (389b1–3) or "what a shuttle itself is (*ho estin kerkis*)" (389b5). The relevant bit of the carpenter's craft, his shuttle-making ability, consists in his being able to put "the nature that naturally best suits it to perform its own work" into some wood (389b3–c7).

Because "there's a type of shuttle that's naturally suited to each type of weaving" (389d1–2), there are shuttles of many different types. Because it is a shuttle's nature that "best suits it to perform its own work" (389b10–c1), it follows that the natures possessed by these different shuttles are themselves different. Moreover, to each of these distinct types of nature, a distinct form corresponds. Hence, the weaver, as we've already seen, knows "whether the *appropriate* form of shuttle is present in any given bit of wood" (390b1–2). But there is also a nature all shuttles have in common: the one that makes them all shuttles. And it is with this less specific nature that the (generic) form of a shuttle is correlated (389a7–8, 389b9–10). Thus, there is an apparent one-to-one correspondence between forms and natures of various levels of specificity.

When a carpenter wants to make a particular type of shuttle what he does is to look to the relevant form and put into some wood the nature that corresponds to it. The resulting shuttle will then have the form (389b8–c1). The rule-setter's activity is modeled exactly on the carpenter's. The carpenter looks to "what a shuttle itself is (*ho estin kerkis*)"; the rule-setter looks to "what a name itself is (*ho estin onoma*)" (389d6–7). A carpenter makes shuttles out of wood by putting into it a nature that copies or imitates a form; a rule-setter makes names out of "sounds and syllables" (389d5–6) or "letters and syllables" (423e8) by putting into them a nature that copies or imitates the form of a name.

Names in general, then, are like shuttles in general: the form of a shuttle (*ho estin kerkis*) is something that all types of shuttles possess; the form of a name (*ho estin onoma*) is what all (correct) names possess. And just as no shuttle is simply a generic shuttle but each is a shuttle of a particular type, so no name is just a generic name but each imitates the being, essence, or form of some specific thing or kind and expresses what it is (423e7–9).

One important consequence of this analogy is that it enables Socrates to introduce with relative ease an account of identity or synonymy for names. For just as two different carpenters can make exactly the same type of shuttle out of different pieces of wood, so two different rule-setters can make exactly the same name out of different sounds or syllables (393c–d). Thus, names must not be confused with the phonic or graphic realizations of them in distinct languages: 'dog', 'kuôn', 'chien', and 'hund' are all the same name. The implied identity or synonymy condition for names is that names are the same or mean the same if they express the same nature. In the course of the dialogue, this somewhat demanding condition will be modified and made more accommodating (§§9, 13).

There is a one-to-one correspondence between natures and forms. Why? How are natures related to forms and how are both related to actual shuttles? Socrates suggests answers but his dialectical purposes do not call for their elaboration. Since forms become important again later in the dialogue, however, in a much more metaphysically-freighted context, it will be useful for us to tease out some of the details he is able to leave unexplored. The maker of a shuttle looks to the form of a shuttle and begins to carve a piece of wood. But the shuttle he is making breaks. Where does he look in making the next one? Not towards the broken one, obviously, but "to the very form to which he looked in making the one he broke" (389b1–3). Why are we told this? Surely, it is to drive home the fact that the form exists "separately" from particular shuttles and so is immune to the vicissitudes to which they are prone. In language soon to become central, individual shuttles may be *in flux*, wearing out or breaking in the process of being made, but the shuttle itself is always such as it is (§12).

Are natures the same as forms? Is their one-to-one correspondence a consequence of their identity? With so little to go on it is difficult to be sure, but there is reason to think that the answer is no. The carpenter's shuttle will have the appropriate form only if he succeeds in putting into it "the nature that naturally best suits it to perform its own work" (389b10–c1). But, of course, he may not succeed completely. If he doesn't, his shuttle will be an imperfect example of a shuttle of the type he is trying to make—not a perfect example of some other type of shuttle. What enables us to say this is the fact that the nature he has put into the shuttle is an imperfect copy of the form he is looking to. (Socrates makes an analogous claim about names at 432d11–433a2.) We seem, then, to be on familiar Platonic ground: particulars participate in forms through possessing natures which resemble those forms. A particular shuttle owes its identity as a shuttle to its nature. Its nature owes its identity to the form it copies. But with the form, indebtedness ends, since it just is "what a shuttle itself is."[5]

I have suggested that Socrates' few brief remarks about forms, amounting to no more that a handful of short sentences, should be seen as a sketch of the much more elaborate picture of forms that we find in, for example, the *Republic*. It might be objected that it is hard to believe that so contentious a theory would be introduced so casually or be accepted without blinking by Hermogenes and Cratylus. But such an objection would be misdirected. What is introduced is a sketch of a contentious theory from which the more contentious parts have been omitted as unneeded for the present argument. It would thus be dialectically inept of Socrates to flaunt them. But, by the same token, it would be hermeneutically inept of us not to detect their shadowy presence even in the sketch.

§5   Homer on the Correctness of Names

By the end of the discussion of name-making, Hermogenes' conventionalist account of the correctness of names has been shown to be incompatible with his realism about things and actions, his realism about truth. If names are like shuttles, and name-making (rule-setting) like carpentry, then

Cratylus is right in saying that things have natural names,

---

5. See my *Philosopher-Kings: The Argument of Plato's Republic* (Princeton, 1988), §2.8.

and that not everyone is a craftsman of names, but only someone who looks to the natural name of each thing and is able to
put its form into letters and syllables. (390d9–e4)

Hermogenes is no more than semi-convinced. He cannot answer
Socrates, but he finds it hard to change his opinion.[6] He would
like to be shown a naturally correct name, so that he can see
what it is for a name to express the nature of a thing. This is a
new topic and is explicitly registered as such. We are clearer
now that "names do possess some sort of natural correctness
and that it isn't every man who knows how to name things
well" (391a8–b2). Our next task is "to try to discover what this
correctness is" (391b4–5).

Socrates suggests that the best way to make this discovery is
to learn it from someone who, unlike himself, has made it already: someone like the sophists. But Hermogenes will have
none of that; as before, despite occasional temptations, he is no
Protagorean. In that case, Socrates tells him, he will have to
"learn [it] from Homer and the other poets" (391c8–d1). The implicit disjunctive syllogism is casually employed, easy to glide
over. Yet it is significant. The poets are the traditional teachers;
the Sophists are the new ones. If we don't learn from one, we
must learn from the other. If Protagoras is out of the question,
Homer, Hesiod, and the other poets will have to be our authori-
ties—though, as in the *Republic*, where poets are bowdlerized by
philosophers, the hidden authority of our own dialectical intelli-
gences will temper their teachings.

Homer "distinguishes between the names humans call things
and those the gods call them" (391d4–6). The gods call them by
their "naturally correct" names (391d8–e1), but it is "too hard"
for humans to figure out in what way these names are naturally
correct (392b1–2). Subtly, a note of epistemic caution is introduced, later it will be sounded more insistently:

The first and finest line of investigation, which as intelligent
people we must acknowledge, is this, that we admit that we
know nothing about the gods themselves or about the names

---

6. In this he is like many of Socrates' interlocutors.

they call themselves—although it is clear that they call themselves by true ones. The second best line on the correctness of names is to say, as is customary in our prayers, that we hope the gods are pleased by the names we give them, since we know no others. I think this is an excellent custom. You would want us, then, to begin our investigation by first announcing to the gods that we will not be investigating *them*—since we do not regard ourselves as worthy to conduct such an investigation—but rather human beings, and the beliefs they had in giving the gods their names. After all, there's no offense in doing that. (400e2–401a5; see *Republic* 427b–c)

Caution applies not when we are investigating human beliefs, but rather when we purport to be investigating the gods themselves or the real natures of things. So when it emerges that we *can* explain the kind of correctness with which some Homeric names are given, that it *is* possible to explain the sort of correctness that belongs to the names 'Skamandrios' and 'Astyanax' (392b3–7), we should infer that this is because we are really investigating human beliefs. The poems of Homer and Hesiod are "stories we tell because we don't know the truth about those ancient events" (*Republic* 382c10–d2). Thus, we are in a realm where human beliefs have authority.

Socrates is assuming, then, that the characters who figure in myths have their natures correctly depicted therein, so that knowledge of the myths provides one with knowledge of these natures. Orestes is portrayed as having a brutal, savage, and rugged nature, so his name is naturally correct, since it expresses his nature (394e). Agamemnon is also correctly named because his name expresses the nature he is presented as having in the Homeric poems (395a–b).

Through investigating these and other names, Socrates uncovers two related principles at work in Homeric nomenclature. The first is the *principle of natural descent*, characterized as "right (*dikaion*)" at 393b7–8: if X is a natural (or non-monstrous) offspring of Y, and Y has a nature of kind F, then X has a nature of kind F and should, like Y, be called by a name that expresses F, otherwise not. Hector is a king (he has a kingly nature); so his natural son, Astyanax, also has a kingly nature. It is this fact that is reflected in their Homeric names; for '*anax*' ('lord') and '*hek-*

tôr' ('possessor') "signify pretty much the same, since both are names for a king" (393a). But if a pious father has an impious son, one whose nature is different from his own, the son should not be given a name like 'Theophilus' ('God-beloved') that expresses a nature he does not have (394e1–6).

Previously, Socrates has talked about forms and natures, now he talks instead about the *dunameis*, the forces or powers, of things and names.[7] It is fairly clear, however, that at least where functionally defined items like names, medicines, and other tools are concerned, powers are pretty much the same as natures. Thus, a name for a letter that includes its force or power expresses its nature (393d6–e8). It is no surprise to find, therefore, that the identity condition for names, earlier expressed in terms of forms or natures, is now expressed in terms of powers. Previously we discovered that two names made up of different sounds or syllables are really the same or signify the same if their natures or forms are the same—natures or forms which, in their cases, are determined by the natures or forms of the things they signify (393d1–4). Now we are told that 'Hector' and 'Astyanax', which don't look at all the same, and have just the letter 't' in common, nonetheless express the same thing because they embody the same force or power (394b2–6). This *sameness of power principle* for individuating names is the second principle that Socrates finds at work in Homer.

The *principle of natural descent* and the *sameness of power principle* are Socrates' Homeric inheritance and provide him with a "sort of outline" (397a5) to follow in the next stage of the investigation.

§6   The Testimony of Names Themselves

So far the investigation has for the most part concerned names whose makers or givers are known. Now it is broadened to focus on other names. The project is to try to determine whether

---

7. In the *Republic*, powers are defined as "a class of the things that are that enable us — or anything else, for that matter — to do whatever we are capable of doing. Sight, for example, and hearing are among the powers, if you understand the kind of thing I'm referring to." (477b–c)

etymological analysis can detect the hand of a maker in them. "Which names," Socrates asks, "do you want us to begin with, in order to find out whether names themselves will testify to us that they are not given by chance, but have some sort of correctness?" (397a4–b1). But although the focus has in one way become broader, in another, it has narrowed. The names given to men and heroes are unlikely to be given correctly, or to embody their powers or express their natures, because they are given for reasons that have little to do with those natures: "they are often given because they are the names of ancestors" or "in the hope that they will prove appropriate" (397b2–5). So they are set aside as unpromising. No sort of correctness is likely to be found in them. Instead, Socrates and Hermogenes will focus on the names of things "that by nature always are (*ta aei onta kai pephukota*), since it is proper for their names to be given with the greatest care, and some may even be the work of a more than human power" (397b7–c2; cf. 438c1–4).

What are these things? What does it mean to characterize them in this way? We may begin with a list of the names subsequently investigated, dividing them into groups that correspond to clearly differentiated stages in the investigation (though in group (6) I have collapsed some of these stages):

(1) NAMES OF THE RATIONAL BEINGS (397c–399b): *'theoi'* ('gods'), *'daimones'* ('daimons'), *'hêrôs'* ('hero'), *'anthrôpoi'* ('humans')

(2) NAMES OF BASIC CONSTITUENTS OF RATIONAL BEINGS (399d–400d): *'psuchê'* ('soul'), *'sôma'* ('body')

(3) NAMES OF INDIVIDUAL PERSONAL GODS (400d–408e): 'Hestia', 'Rhea', 'Kronos', etc.

(4) NAMES OF COSMOLOGICAL GODS (408e–410e): *'hêlios'* ('sun'), *'meis'* ('month'), *'pur'* ('fire'), *'hudôr'* ('water'), *'aêr'* ('air'), *'hôrai'* ('seasons'), etc.

(5) NAMES OF THE MORAL AND INTELLECTUAL VIRTUES OR POWERS (411a–413e): *'phronêsis'* ('wisdom'), *'gnômê'* ('judgment'), *'skopein'* ('examining'), *'noêsis'* ('understanding'), *'sôphrosunê'* ('moderation'), *'epistêmê'* ('knowledge'), *'sunesis'* ('comprehension'), *'sophia'* ('wisdom'), *'agathon'* ('good'), *'dikaiosunê'* ('justice'), *'dikaion'* ('just'), *'andreia'* ('courage')

(6) NAMES OF MORAL, EPISTEMIC, AND PRUDENTIAL VALUES AND DIS-

VALUES (414b–420d): *'technê'* ('craft'), *'mêchanê'* ('contrivance'), *'aretê'* ('virtue') and *'kakia'* ('vice'), *'deilia'* ('cowardice'), *'aporia'* ('perplexity'), *'kakon'* ('bad'), *'kalon'* ('fine', 'beautiful'), *'aischron'* ('disgraceful', 'ugly'), *'sumpheron'* ('advantageous'), *'kerdaleon'* ('gainful'), *'lusiteloun'* ('profitable'), *'ôphelimon'* ('beneficial'), *'blaberon'* ('harmful') and *'zêmiôdes'* ('hurtful'), *'deon'* ('obligation'), *'hêdonê'* ('pleasure'), *'lupê'* ('pain'), *'ania'* ('sorrow'), *'algêdôn'* ('distress'), *'odunê'* ('grief'), *'achthêdôn'* ('affliction'), *'chara'* ('joy'), *'erpsis'* ('delight'), *'euphrosunê'* ('lightheartedness'), *'epithumia'* ('appetite'), *'thumos'* ('spirit', 'anger'), *'himeros'* ('desire'), *'pothos'* ('longing'), *'erôs'* ('erotic love'), *'doxa'* ('opinion'), *'oiêsis'* ('thinking'), *'boulê'* ('planning'), *'boulesthai'* ('wishing'), *'bouleuesthai'* ('deliberating'), *'aboulia'* ('lack of planning'), *'hekousion'* ('voluntary'), *'anagkê'* ('compulsion')[8]

(7) "THE FINEST AND MOST IMPORTANT NAMES" (421a–c): *'onoma'* ('name'), *'alêtheia'* ('truth'), *'pseudos'* ('falsehood'), *'on'* or *'ousia'* ('being')

(8) "THE PRIMARY NAMES" (421c–427d): *'ion'* ('going'), *'rheon'* ('flowing'), and *'doun'* ('shackling'), *'rhoê'* ('flowing'), and *'schesis'* ('restraining')

The names listed in (5) through (8) are pretty clearly names of things that "always are," because they are names of forms, which exist always and are unchanging (439a10–440d6). The things whose names appear in (1) through (4), on the other hand, seem not to be forms, since Plato does not ever admit forms of particulars, such as Rhea or the sun. Presumably, then, the phrase *ta aei onta kai pephukota* is somewhat broad in conno-

---

8. David Sedley, "The Etymologies in Plato's *Cratylus*," forthcoming in the *Journal of Hellenic Studies* (1999), astutely notices the importance of the inclusion of *'hekousion'* and *'anagkê'* in this list. He writes: "We tend to think of the ethical issue which these represent, that of the voluntary nature of moral action, as one first put on the map by Aristotle and not fully investigated until the Hellenistic age. But here we have a clear indication that Plato considered it a proper ethical topic. As it happens, none of the dialogues preserves his discussion of it, but here we have a salutary reminder that not all Plato's philosophical work found its way into his published dialogues."

tation, referring to those entities (including forms) that are by nature always present in the cosmos.[9]

Look now at (7) and (8). Why are the names in them characterized as they are? Those in (7) are presumably "the finest and most important" because the forms they name are both fundamental to philosophy, especially to the philosophical account of names that Socrates and Hermogenes have already sketched. But what about those in (8), why are they "the primary names"? The answer lies in the brief methodological prelude to the discussion of the names in (3). There Socrates claims that "the first name-givers weren't ordinary people, but lofty thinkers and subtle reasoners" (401b6–8), who "all lean towards the doctrines of Heraclitus" (402c2–3). In other words, they all believe that things are all flowing like rivers, all in flux. Hence, the names included in (8) are primary because they are the fundamental terms in the metaphysical theory of reality presupposed by the first name-givers: "It's clear that the first name-giver gave names to things based on his conception of what those things were like" (436b5–7). Thus all the names in (1) through (8) signify the being or essence of things to us *on the assumption that all things are moving and flowing and being swept along* (436e2–5). Remember that a cognate assumption is in operation in the discussion of Homer and the poets.

Once we see why the names in (8) are primary, something else becomes clear, namely, that there is nothing haphazard in the list of names Socrates selects for investigation. They are all of fundamental philosophical importance: they are the key terms of theology, cosmology, metaphysics, epistemology, philosophy of mind, and ethics. Hence a philosophical theory of reality as a whole owes us an account of them that is couched exclusively in terms of the names of the things it takes to be primary. That is why, in the discussion which follows, Socrates gives accounts of all these names in terms of motion or flow. If

---

9. See Catherine Dalimier, *Platon Cratyle*, 219–220 n. 120: "La suite montre que la formule désigne au moins les dieux et des puissances divines, par opposition des hommes; mais elle est suffisamment général pour englober d'autres êtres éternels, dont nous savons déjà qu'ils mêritant de vrais noms, les êtres en soi, c'est à dire les formes."

they were in fact given by Heraclitean name-givers, as he is supposing, this enterprise must prove successful.

It is precisely because the enterprise *must* prove successful, indeed, that Socrates is entitled to engage in what must otherwise seem to be wholly illegitimate tactics. He adds and subtracts letters from names (399a, 400b–c, 414c), offers different candidate accounts as equally plausible (402d–403a, 407a–c), represents some names as distorted by our greater interest in euphony than truth (404d, 414c–d, 418b–c), others as foreign imports that can be set aside (410a–b), and adopts auxiliary hypotheses of his own pretty much at will (403b–404b, 406b–d). He does all these in full awareness of the risks of arbitrariness they involve: "if we can add whatever we like to names, or subtract whatever we like from them, it will be far too easy to fit any name to any thing" (414d7–9). But he also does it with justification. For he is supposing that he knows the intention with which the names were originally given, and so can (within limits) represent apparent failures to carry it out as mistakes on the part of the first name-givers themselves (436c7–d3), or as the results of subsequent distortions introduced by others.

What is most important from the philosophical point of view in these etymologies, then, is this: (1) they are of a sort that must be correct, if names were originally given by Heraclitean theorists; (2) they therefore provide an illustration of what names would have to be like if they were given on the basis of a correct theory of the natures of things and of reality (though Socrates certainly does not think, as we shall see, that correct names must imitate reality in the crude way that the etymologies themselves suggest).

§7   The Etymologies

While for us the etymologies have largely illustrative significance, their significance to Plato's contemporaries may well have been different. We typically do not expect to find a solution to philosophical problems in etymology, and so do not need to be shown in detail why we shouldn't; they perhaps did. The *Cratylus* certainly places Euthyphro and Cratylus in that unhappy boat. Is it justified in doing so? We do not know, since we have very little information about these men other than what Plato's own dialogues tell us.

We know, to be sure, that Greek thinkers and writers often make use of etymology for one purpose or another, sometimes suggesting that names have a mystical significance that provides important clues to the fates of their bearers. In Aeschylus' *Agamemnon* (681–90), for instance, the name 'Helen' is treated as though the first part derived from the root *'Hele-'* ('to kill', 'to destroy'). In Sophocles' *Ajax* (430–3), the tragic Ajax connects his own name *'Aias'* ('Ajax') to the expression of woe *'aias'* ('alas'). In *Oedipus Tyrannus* (1033–6), 'Oedipus' is taken to derive from *'oidein'* ('to swell') and *'pous'* ('foot'), as it is in Euripides' *Phoenician Women* (21). Philosophers too produce similar arguments from time to time. In the *Phaedrus*, Socrates cites the etymological derivation of *'erôs'* ('love') from *'rhômê'* ('strength') as evidence of the power of love (238c2–3). And in *De Caelo*, Aristotle borrows with approval the derivation (410b) of *'aithêr'* ('either') from *'thein aei'* ('running always').[10] Moreover, the *Cratylus* itself refers to two different series of lectures on the correctness of names given by the sophist Prodicus of Ceos (384b2–c1, also *Euthydemus* 277e3–4).[11] But we have little direct evidence of any *systematic* philosophical employment of etymology or etymologically-based arguments prior to Plato's own rather complexly-motivated kind in the *Cratylus*.

Nonetheless, it is surely hard to believe that Plato took such pains to refute a straw man. For not only does he provide etymological details that go well beyond the needs of mere illustration, but many of these details seem to draw on etymologies seriously proposed by others. For example, Aristotle (*De Anima* 405^{b}26–9) refers to thinkers who "construct etymologies" in which they derive *'psuchê'* ('soul') from *'katapsuchein'* ('to cool down'). The derivation of *'psuchê'* from *'anapsuchon'* may well be a sly reference to these thinkers (399d–e). Similarly, the deriva-

---

10. See also *Nicomachean Ethics* 1103^{a}17–18, 1132^{a}30–32. I was reminded of these Platonic and Aristotelian appeals to etymology by David Sedley, "The Etymologies in Plato's *Cratylus*."
11. Prodicus is also mentioned in *Protagoras* 337a1–c4, *Meno* 75e, *Laches* 197d, *Charmides* 163a–b.

tion of *'sôma'* from *'sêma'* ('tomb') may derive from Heraclitus or (as is perhaps more likely) from the Pythagoreans.[12]

Though very little is certain in all of this,[13] it does seem reasonable to believe that in addition to using the etymologies for illustrative philosophical purposes of his own, Plato is also using them to criticize or parody specific individual thinkers who use etymological arguments in philosophy without showing any awareness of the problematic presuppositions of doing so. It is perhaps also reasonable to believe, as Socrates' admission that "the name-givers really did give them in the belief that everything is always moving and flowing" (439c1–4) suggests, that Plato takes some of the etymologies seriously as etymologies or as correctly reflecting the thoughts of the ancient name-givers.[14] But there we must surely stop. For even if these name-givers correctly named some things, so that some things are genuinely in flux, Socrates is adamant that etymology is in general a poor guide to the natures of things (440c1–d7).

A key example is the priceless moment at which Socrates exhibits his willingness to re-run some etymologies on principles opposite to the Heraclitean ones he first adopts (436e–437c). Of the names he now considers, only *'epistêmê'* ('knowledge') has already been analyzed, but the conclusion he reaches seems quite general: if *any* "names of excellent things" have credible non-Heraclitean etymologies, then none of the names that "signify motion" can be assumed to be true. This shows, surely, both how little Plato has *philosophically* invested in the original Heraclitean etymologies, and how easy it is—absent constraints imposed on names by an independent investigation of nature—to make names tell whatever philosophical story one wishes.

For Plato's contemporaries, then, the attack on etymology-based philosophy may have brought its own special delights or

---

12. See Plato, *Gorgias* 493a1–b3, and E. R. Dodds, *Plato Gorgias* (Oxford, 1959), 300.

13. As a glance at the admirably sober discussion in T. M. S. Baxter, *The Cratylus: Plato's Critique of Naming* (Leiden, 1992), Chs. 4–5, eloquently attests.

14. See David Sedley, "The Etymologies in Plato's *Cratylus*," and Rachel Barney, *A Reading of Plato's Cratylus* (Unpublished Ph.D. dissertation, Princeton University 1996).

agonies, but for us little is philosophically at stake in them. So we should not, as philosophically-motivated readers, allow ourselves to become bogged down in their details.

§8   Primary Names

After about twenty-five pages of analysis, of taking apart what the primary name-givers put together (425a5–b3), all the non-primary names in (1) through (7) are taken to have been successfully resolved into the primary ones in (8). However, the primary ones cannot be investigated by being analyzed into still other names (422a1–b8). Yet a primary name's correctness, like that of a non-primary one, *is* a matter of "expressing the nature of one of the things that are," of making it "as clear as possible to us" (422d11–e1). Moreover, "if one doesn't know about the correctness of primary names, one cannot know about the correctness of derivative ones, which can only express something by means of those others about which one knows nothing" (426a6–b3). Much, therefore, hangs on the account of primary names.[15] Socrates' discussion of them is partly carried out with Hermogenes, partly with Cratylus. I shall draw on it as a whole.

Primary names imitate not the qualities of things (such as their colors or sounds), as music and painting sometimes do, but their being or essence. They do this by being composed of letters and syllables that imitate, by naturally resembling, the essences they are applied to by the name-giver (422e–425c, 433d–434a). These letters and syllables are not names, but elements of names, which stand to names much as pigments do to paintings (434a–b).[16]

An example will help explain what Socrates has in mind. On the assumption that the first name-givers were Heracliteans, the name *'agathon'* ('good') might be analyzed into two other names *'agaston'* ('admirable') and *'thoon'* ('fast'). *'Thoon'* might then be further analyzed into the primary names *'rhoê'* ('flowing') plus some other primary or non-primary names, and similarly for

15. Plato returns to the problem of our knowledge of primary names at *Theaetetus* 201c–210d.
16. See Norman Kretzmann, "Plato on the Correctness of Names," *American Philosophical Quarterly* 8 (1971), 126–38.

'*agaston*'. Now what makes the non-primary name '*agathon*' a name of goodness isn't that it naturally resembles the nature of goodness, but rather that all the primary names into which it is resolved are assigned by the name-giver to elemental components of the nature of goodness that they naturally resemble. For example, '*rhoê*' is a primary name of flowing because the letter '*rho*' ('r') in it naturally resembles motion, since the tongue is "most agitated and least at rest in pronouncing this letter" (426e4–5).

What is Socrates' attitude to the theory he explores in such detail? To answer we need to distinguish its various aspects. First, Socrates does genuinely favor accounts, like the Heraclitean one, in which names are assigned by name-givers on the basis of their knowledge of the natures of things (§13). Second, he seems to believe that any account of the correctness of names will have to distinguish primary names from derivative ones (424b7–425c3), and apply to both in the same way (422c7–9). Consequently, the Homeric principle of natural descent does turn out to be genuinely fundamental to the correctness of names. For if derivative names are to be correct, they must be natural descendants of elementary names, in just the way that what they name must be natural descendants of the elementary components of their natures. But Socrates does not believe, as we saw in §1, that any account of the correctness of names can, like the Heraclitean one, leave convention out of the picture altogether (435c2–6).

Neither does Socrates believe that the various analyses of names he produces are guaranteed to be correct. One way he signals this is by representing the wisdom that enables him to produce them as alien and suspect, as something that must later be exorcised:

I, for my part, mostly blame Euthyphro, of the deme of Prospalta, for its [this wisdom's] coming upon me. I was with him at dawn, lending an ear to his lengthy discussion. He must have been inspired, because it looks as though he has not only filled my ears with his superhuman wisdom but taken possession of my soul as well. So it seems to me that this is what we ought to do: Today, we'll use this wisdom and finish our examination of names, but tomorrow, if the rest of you agree, we'll exorcise it and purify ourselves, as soon as we've found someone—whether priest or wise man—who is clever at that kind of purification. (396d4–397a1)

Later, as he is about to begin his discussion with Cratylus, he provides an important clue to the nature of the exorcism he has in mind:

> But, Cratylus, *I* have long been surprised at my own wisdom —and doubtful of it, too. That's why I think it's necessary to keep reinvestigating whatever I say, since self-deception is the worst thing of all. How could it not be terrible, indeed, when the deceiver never deserts you even for an instant but is always right there with you? Therefore, I think we have to turn back frequently to what we've already said, in order to test it by looking at it "backwards and forwards simultaneously," as the aforementioned poet [Homer] puts it. So, let's now see what we *have* said. (428d1–e2)

This suggests that it is dialectical examination that will provide the needed exorcism, an exorcism that is indeed begun, as we shall see, in the discussion with Cratylus.

Moreover, Socrates does not accept the Heraclitean theory that the first name-givers are being supposed to have adopted. Indeed, he represents Heracliteanism, not as the truth about reality, but as the projection on to it of intellectual confusion:

> Most of our wise men nowadays get so dizzy going around and around in their search for the nature of the things that are, that the things themselves appear to them to be turning around and moving every which way. Well, I think that the people who gave things their names in very ancient times are exactly like these wise men. They don't blame this on their own internal condition, however, but on the nature of the things themselves, which they think are never stable or steadfast, but flowing and moving, full of every sort of motion and constant coming into being. (411b3–c6)

A little later, he implicitly connects this confusion too with the inability of these wise men to produce accounts that are stable under dialectical examination, rather than exhibiting the intellectual equivalent of flux:

> Even when I'd heard this [account of justice], however, I persisted in gently asking, "If all this is true, my friend, what actually *is* the just?" Thereupon, they think I am asking too many questions and demanding the impossible, and they tell me that I have already learned enough. Then they try to satisfy me by having each tell me his own view. But they disagree with each other. One says that the just is the sun . . . [another] says that it is fire (*to pur*)—but that isn't easy to understand. Another says that it isn't fire, but the heat itself that is in fire. Another says that all these explanations are ridiculous, and that the just is what Anaxagoras talks about, namely, mind . . . Thereupon, my friend, I am even more perplexed than when I set out to learn what the just is. (413a5–d1)

Since in the initial discussion with Hermogenes genuine authority in using and giving names was ascribed to the dialectician, it is hardly surprising that errors in name-giving should be laid at the door of dialectical inadequacy. But because of the subsequent disappearance of the dialectician from center stage after his initial brief appearance there (§1), it is important to bear his shadowy re-emergence in mind (see §13).

§9   Cratylus on Truth, Falsity, and Fitting

Cratylus accepts without scruple the entire Heraclitean theory of names that Socrates, inspired by Euthyphro, has developed (428b6–c8). He also accepts some of the results of the earlier examination of Hermogenes: he agrees that "the correctness of a name consists in displaying the nature of the thing it names" (428e1–2), and that the craft that gives names to things is the craft of the rule-setter (429a1, 388d9–389a3). What he does not accept is that rule-setters, like other craftsmen, can make mistakes and produce names that do not fit natures perfectly (429b1–11). Names are keys. So if a name fits something, it is its name, but if it doesn't, it isn't (429c3–5).

Mistakes could still be possible, however, since rule-setters who made wholly correct names could nonetheless misassign all of them, never giving a name that correctly expresses a nature to anything that has that nature. To preserve his account, therefore, Cratylus must show that this is not a genuine possibility at all. His attempt to do so introduces an old Sophistic standby: a name cannot be misapplied because "false speaking is in every way impossible" (429d1–2).[17] For how, he asks, "can anyone say the thing he says and not say something that is? Doesn't speaking falsely consist in not saying things that are?" (429d4–6). Socrates' trenchant response is first directed against this Parmenidean-sounding argument, then against the claim that names are keys.[18]

Cratylus agrees that names are imitations of things:[19] they are not paintings—they resemble a thing's nature, not its qualities—but they are *like* paintings (430a10–b4). He also agrees that a painting can be assigned (*dianomê*) to something of which it is an imitation or to something of which it isn't, that one can step up to a man and say "This is your portrait," while showing him "what happens to be his own likeness, or what happens to be the likeness of a woman" (430e3–6). Similarly, one can say to a man "Your name is 'man'" or "Your name is 'woman'." When the name or picture does not fit what it is assigned to, the assignment is incorrect; but only in the case of names is it also false (430d1–7).[20] Hence, though Cratylus is reluctant to agree that names can be misassigned (430d8–e2), he accepts that if they can, they can also be false of their nominata (430d8–431c3). Maybe the name 'Hermogenes' means 'of the family of Hermes' and designates someone just in case he is of that family, but a speaker can apply 'Hermogenes' to someone who is or to some-

---

17. Nicholas Denyer, *Language, Thought, and Falsehood in Ancient Greek Philosophy* (London, 1991), explores the arguments for this claim, and the attempts made by various ancient philosophers to refute them.

18. See Parmenides of Elea, Fragments B.2–8, translated and discussed in Richard D. McKirahan, Jr., *Philosophy Before Socrates* (Indianapolis, 1994), 151–174.

19. What he really holds is that elementary names naturally resemble primary natures, see 431c4–d8, §13.

20. See Bernard Williams, "Cratylus' Theory of Names," in Malcolm Schofield and Martha Nussbaum (eds.), *Language and Logos* (Cambridge, 1982), especially 87–89.

one who isn't of that family, and succeed in both referring to him and saying something false of him. Since both names and verbs can be false in this way, so can statements, since they are "a combination of names and verbs" (431b4–c1). Thus the Parmenidean obstacle that Cratylus raised to speaking falsely, and so to the rule-setter's misassigning correctly constructed names to things, has been demolished.

Cratylus is next made to back away from his claim that names are keys. Primary names are (relevantly) like paintings. And in paintings "it's possible to present all the appropriate colors and shapes" or to leave some out or add some inappropriate ones. In the first case, the painting is a good likeness, in the second, though it is still a likeness, it is a bad one (431c4–d13). Cratylus initially resists the extension of this analogy to primary names:

> But you see, Socrates, when we assign '*a*', '*b*', and each of the other letters to names by using the craft of grammar, if we add, subtract, or transpose a letter, we don't simply write the name incorrectly, we don't write *it* at all, for it immediately becomes a different name, if any of those things happens. (431e9–432a4)

But Socrates overcomes his resistance:

> What you say may well be true of numbers, which have to be a certain number or not be at all. For example, if you add anything to the number ten or subtract anything from it, it immediately becomes a different number, and the same is true of any other number you choose. But this isn't the sort of correctness that belongs to things with sensory qualities, such as images in general. Indeed, the opposite is true of them—an image cannot remain an image if it presents all the details of what it represents. (432a8–b4)

An *exact* image of Cratylus wouldn't be his name, Socrates claims, but another Cratylus.

Socrates' point is this. Cratylus holds that two primary names are the same if and only if they are exactly the same

string of letters. It is this view that Socrates quite rightly rejects.
Here is the key passage:

> Consider numbers, Cratylus, since you want to have recourse
> to them. Where do you think you'll get names that are like
> each one of the numbers, if you don't allow this agreement
> and convention of yours to have some control over the cor-
> rectness of names? (435b6–c2)

Because there are an infinite number of natural numbers, but a
finite number of elementary names (letters or syllables of the alphabet), whatever names we use for the numbers must be recursively constructible from a finite base set of names. We have ten
such names:

$$\text{'0', '1', '2', \ldots '9'.}$$

We employ these names to construct the names of each of the
subsequent numbers according to a rule:

$$\text{'10', '11' \ldots '20' \ldots '30', \ldots '300', \ldots}$$

The Greeks use different names and a different rule. They begin
with the number one and name it and the next nine natural
numbers using their alphabet as follows:

$$\alpha', \beta', \gamma' \ldots, \iota'.$$

They use these names to name the other numbers through nineteen:

$$\iota\alpha' \ (11), \iota\beta' \ (12), \ldots, \iota\theta' \ (19).$$

Then they use the remaining letters of the alphabet, for the
twenties, thirties, and so on, through the eight hundreds:

$$\kappa' \ (20), \ldots \lambda' \ (30), \ldots \tau' \ (300), \ldots \omega' \ (800).$$

Since there seems to be no credible way to argue that one of
these ways of naming the numbers is more correct (as opposed

to easier to manipulate), or that either is more correct than the Roman system of numerals, or than names constructed out of '1' and '0' in base two, Socrates' conclusion seems secured. The names '19', 'ιθ', and 'XIX' all name the number nineteen, but they are not the same string of letters.[21]

As a result of this argument, Cratylus is brought to accept that other Homeric principle, the sameness of power principle (393d2–4; §5), now expressed in terms of patterns instead of powers. A name "will describe the thing well, if it includes all the appropriate letters"; but it need not describe it well in order to be its name: "it will still describe the thing if it includes its pattern (*tupos*)" (432e3–433b5). Once Cratylus accepts this principle, he must abandon his view that names are keys. A key cannot open a (good) lock unless it fits it exactly, but a name can fit a thing and be its name, even if it doesn't fit it exactly. Under dialectical examination, therefore, Cratylus' theory, like Hermogenes', undergoes substantial modification.

§10 Convention Returns

Cratylus' theory undergoes substantial modification, but not, it may seem, as substantial as that undergone by Hermogenes's. After all, Hermogenes began by claiming that names function as conventional tags and that dubbing always trumps fitting. But he was brought to concede that fitting, in the shape of the sameness of power principle, also has a role to play in the correctness of names. Cratylus began by claiming that names are keys (perfect natural fits for their nominata), and that fitting always trumps dubbing. He was forced to agree that names are not keys, not perfect fits. He too is brought to accept the sameness of power principle. But has he had to acknowledge that convention or *dubbing* has a role to play in the correctness of names? We have seen in passing that he has; Socrates' argument about the names of the numbers establishes that. But it is just a clinching coda to his main argument.

Cratylus thinks that the original name-givers were Heracliteans, that they were right about the nature of things, and that

---

those natures are recoverable through analysis of the names we actually use (436d2–4). He agrees that "a name is a way of expressing a thing" (433d1–2), that all names are either primary or derivative (433d4–5), and that primary names fit things because the letters or elements from which they are composed are "naturally like" the elements of the natures of those things (434a3–5). Thus he thinks that Socrates was "right to say that '*r*' is like motion, moving, and hardness" and that "'*l*' is like smoothness, softness, and the other things we mentioned" (434c1–5). The problem Socrates raises for these views is one that is foreshadowed in the very opening of the dialogue, when Hermogenes reports Cratylus as claiming that his name isn't 'Hermogenes'. What Socrates does is to ask Cratylus about the name '*sklêrotês*' ('hardness'), in which both an appropriate '*r*' and an inappropriate '*l*' are included. Given the views he accepts, Cratylus ought to understand this name as meaning both hardness and softness or neither. Instead, he knows exactly what it means (434e1–3), just as he knows that 'Hermogenes' refers to Hermogenes. To explain how he can know what his theory entails that he cannot know, he appeals to convention (434e4–435a1). In other words, he is forced to take a leaf from Hermogenes' book, just as Hermogenes was earlier forced to take a leaf, though a modified one, from his.

He is not alone in suffering this fate. For, as we know, Socrates himself thinks that any account of the correctness of names will have to make use of convention:

Even if usage is completely different from convention, still you must say that expressing something isn't a matter of likeness but of usage, since usage, it seems, enables both like and unlike names to express things. Since we agree on these points, Cratylus, for I take your silence as a sign of agreement, both convention and usage must contribute something to expressing what we mean when we speak. . . . I myself prefer the view that names should be as much like things as possible, but I fear that defending this view is like hauling a ship up a sticky ramp, as Hermogenes suggested, and that we have to make use of this worthless thing, convention, in the correctness of names. For probably the best possible way to speak consists in using names all (or most) of which are like the things they name (that is, are appropriate to them), while the worst is to use the opposite kind of names. (435a10–d1)

The trouble is that this argument threatens to accomplish too much. For if someone who believes in the natural correctness of names must also make use of convention, why can't convention alone do *all* the work, as Hermogenes initially argued? Cratylus and Socrates might almost seem to be admitting that it can. When Cratylus tells his apparently strange story about 'Hermogenes' not being Hermogenes' name, he puts the matter like this: "People take it (*dokein*) to have been given to him, but it is really the name of someone else, namely, the very one who also has the nature" (429c3–5). Later, Socrates makes a cognate point: "if when I utter a name, you know what I mean, doesn't that name become a way for me to express it to you?" (435a2–3). But if people take 'Hermogenes' to be Hermogenes' name, if they know to whom we're referring when we utter it, what does it matter whether or not it correctly expresses his nature? And surely all that is needed to ensure that they do have this knowledge is that they know the conventions of usage we are following. Convention seems to have returned with a vengeance, then, threatening to make the entire discussion of the natural correctness of names seem beside the point.

§11 Knowledge and Instruction

Having concluded that an account of the correctness of names must make use of convention, Socrates next raises the question, earlier discussed with Hermogenes, of what the function of names is. "Let me next ask you this," he says. "What power do names have for us? What's the good of them?" (435d1–3). Cratylus responds: "To give instruction" (435d4). It is the same response that Socrates himself argued for earlier (388b10–11). But Cratylus holds a much more extreme view, as we saw (§1). He believes that "anyone who knows a thing's name also knows the thing" (435d4–6), and that it is only through names that we can give instruction "about the things that are" or investigate or discover their natures (435e6–436a8).

It is because names are "tools of instruction" about things with natures of their own that Hermogenean conventionalism cannot be the whole truth about their correctness. For names do not serve only as tools of reference, something that contentless tags could conceivably do, they also serve to instruct us about the natures of things, about the way the world is. Ordinary English proper names often provide some such instruction: if I know that your only child's name is 'Mary', I know you have a daughter, not a son. Common names or nouns, such as 'igloo', usually provide even more: when I look up 'igloo' in the dictionary, I find out what that word means, but also, it seems, what an igloo actually is, what its nature is. It is this last fact, no doubt, that makes Cratylus' view somewhat intelligible. But Socrates is aware of the subtle error it involves. "It's clear," he says, "that the first name-giver gave names to things based on his conception of what those things were like." Cratylus agrees. "And if his conception was incorrect and he gave names based on it," Socrates then asks, "what do you suppose will happen to us if we take him as our guide? Won't we be deceived?" (436b5–11). Cratylus' response, after a nostalgic reiteration of his discredited theory that names cannot be assigned incorrectly, is to give, what he calls, a "powerful proof," that "the name-giver didn't miss the truth" (436c2–3). This proof is a consistency argument. Analysis has revealed, he claims, that *all* names are based on the same Heraclitean assumption about the nature of reality, and are all "entirely consistent" with one another.

Socrates is unimpressed with this response for two reasons. First, consistency alone is no proof of truth, because it cannot establish that the first (Heraclitean) principles are true. That is why "every man must think a lot about the first principles of anything and investigate them thoroughly to see whether or not it's correct to assume them" (436d4–6). In the *Republic* this investigation is pegged as one of the tasks of dialectic (510c–511d). Second, Socrates doubts the consistency to which Cratylus appeals. A reexamination of some of the names analyzed earlier, he argues, shows that there are equally plausible analyses of them "from which one could conclude that the name-giver intended to signify not that things were moving and being swept along, but the opposite, that they were at rest" (437a2–c8).

But even if the name-giver did know the natures of the things he named, as Cratylus believes, it still would not follow that the best or only way to discover those natures is through the analysis of names. After all, the name-giver cannot have learned the correctness of primary names in that way, since they cannot be further analyzed into names (438a8–b3). Instead, Socrates suggests that it is better to investigate things and "learn about them through themselves than to do so through their names" (439b4–8). Having first learned the natures of things in this way, it will then be possible to make correct names for them, not otherwise: this is precisely how structural descriptive names, such as 'H_2SO_4', are introduced into chemistry. Knowledge of natures that is not language mediated must thus precede the correct naming of them, as Hermogenes' theory, but not Cratylus', requires (433e2–5). The status of names as tools of *instruction* and *not* primarily of investigation or discovery is confirmed.

§12 Heracliteanism

One important component of Cratylus' theory has thus far remained largely unscathed: his Heracliteanism.[22] In the last pages of the dialogue, it too comes in for examination. Socrates agrees with Cratylus that the name-givers did give many of the philosophically significant names he himself analyzed earlier "in the belief that everything is always moving and flowing." But was their belief correct, or have "the name-givers themselves fallen into a kind of vortex and are whirled around in it dragging us with them"? (439b10–d1; cf. 411b3–c6) The answer, Socrates thinks, hinges on whether or not there are forms and on whether or not *they* are in flux:

> Are we or aren't we to say that there is a beautiful itself, and a good itself, and the same for each one of the things that are?—

---

22. Heraclitus is notoriously difficult to understand. Some of my own views on him are expressed in "Ekpurôsis and the Priority of Fire in Heraclitus," *Phronesis* 27 (1982), 209–305; Charles Kahn, *The Art and Thought of Heraclitus* (Cambridge, 1979) is an excellent translation and full-scale discussion. Plato's Heracliteanism is doubly difficult: see T. H. Irwin, "Plato's Heracleiteanism," *Philosophical Quarterly* 27 (1977), 1–13, Charles Kahn, "Plato and Heraclitus," *Proceedings of the Boston Area Colloquium in Ancient Philosophy* I (1985), 241–58.

I think we are, Socrates.—Let's not investigate whether a particular face or something of that sort is beautiful then, or whether all such things seem to be flowing, but let's ask this instead: Are we to say that the beautiful itself is always such as it is? (439c7–d6)

We already know what Socrates thinks: in his examination of Hermogenes' theory he has claimed that the forms are the stable and unchanging things to which a name-maker or a shuttle-maker looks in the process of making names or shuttles whose natures imitate those forms. Cratylus also accepts this answer. He agrees that there are forms, and that each of them is "always such as it is" (439d5–6). The unchanging Heraclitean etymologies he accepts commit him to doing so. For he accepts that 'knowledge' (*'epistêmê'*) is a naturally correct name that unchangingly indicates or expresses a form that is itself unchanging, namely, the following (*hepetai*) by the soul of the nature of things (412a1–2). The question is whether this commitment is consistent with his view that Heracliteanism provides the best account of reality as a whole, including names and their correctness.

If each form is in flux, "can we correctly say of it first that it is *this*, and then that it is *such and such*?" (439d8–9). In other words, can we combine names (*onomata*) and verbs (*rhemata*) in the way required to make a true statement about it (431b5–c2)? Naming something correctly is not simply a matter of dubbing it with a Hermogenean tag whose descriptive content (if any) is semantically inert or irrelevant. For to name something correctly, one must divide its nature. And what performs this task is the descriptive content of the name, which expresses the pattern of that nature. Thus, 'male human being of the family of Hermes', which is the descriptive content of 'Hermogenes', serves to express the pattern of Hermogenes' nature in the manner requisite for dubbing.

If this is right, it does seem that a flowing subject cannot be dubbed. For how can one dub something in this way that "at the very instant we are speaking," is "inevitably and immediately becoming a different thing and altering and no longer being as it was" (439d10–11)? But if one can never truly say of something that "It *is* this," how can it *be* anything? "After all, if it ever stays the same, it clearly isn't changing—at least, not during that time"

(439e1–3). And if, like the beautiful itself and the other forms, "it always stays the same and is always the same thing, so that it never departs from its own form, how can it ever change or move?" (439e3–5). It seems to follow that the forms are not in flux, and that Heracliteanism, taken as a doctrine about reality as a whole, is false, since it is false of the very forms to which its own account of the correctness of names commits it.

Socrates' final attack on Cratylus' Heracliteanism concerns knowledge. If forms are always changing, they cannot be known, since "at the very instant the knower-to-be approaches, what he is approaching is becoming a different thing, of a different character, so that he can't yet come to know either what sort of thing it is or what it is like" (439e7–440a2). Worse than that, there cannot even *be* knowledge, whether of forms or of anything else. For "if the very form of knowledge passed on from being knowledge, the instant it passed on into a different form than that of knowledge, there would be no knowledge. And if it were always passing on, there would always be no knowledge" (440a9–b4). Thus, if knowledge is in flux, Cratylus' Heracliteanism is epistemically self-refuting: it purports to be something, knowledge, that cannot exist if it is true (440c6–8). On the other hand, if it tries to avoid this unattractive fate by denying that the form of knowledge is in flux, then it is false that everything is in flux, since knowledge isn't (440a7–9).

Socrates concludes that Heraclitus is at least wrong about the forms: they are not "at all like flowings or motions" (440b4–c1). But he is diffident, though no doubt somewhat ironically so, about how securely he has established this conclusion: the truth about the things that are is no easy matter to investigate (440c1–3, 439b4–8). He is more confident, however, that he has at least shown that "no one with any understanding will commit himself or the cultivation of his soul to names, or trust them and their givers to the point of firmly stating that he knows something, nor will he condemn both himself and the things that are as totally unsound and all flowing like leaky pots" (440c3–8).

How successful is this Socratic argument? As with one of its predecessors (§10), one might think that it threatens to be too successful, that it threatens Socrates' own theory as much as Heraclitus'. In a later dialogue, the *Sophist*, Plato puts his finger on the problem as follows (248a–e). When a knower comes to know something he didn't know before, it acquires a property that it previously lacked: the property of being known by him. Hence, when it comes to be known, it seems to undergo change, since change consists in acquiring new properties or losing old ones. It follows that forms are either changeable (in which case Socrates' theory is false and Heracliteanism is somewhat rehabilitated) or unknowable (in which case Socrates' own theory is epistemically self-refuting).

This difficult problem is solved in the *Sophist* by dint of distinguishing a form's intrinsic properties from its extrinsic ones.[23] The property of coming to be known by some knower is an extrinsic property of a form, not one essential to it. So when a form acquires it, the form doesn't intrinsically change, it simply acquires a new extrinsic property it previously lacked. Thus, while wholly unchanging forms are indeed unknowable, forms that do not undergo intrinsic change can be known.

It may be that Plato was aware of this puzzle about forms when he wrote the *Cratylus* and wanted to get us to discover it for ourselves by bringing us within a hair's breadth of it.[24] It may even be that he did not yet know how to solve the puzzle himself. But, whatever about that, Socrates can refute Cratylus by appeal to forms that do not undergo intrinsic change when they come to be known. He doesn't need forms that are so unchanging, even in their extrinsic properties, as to be unknowable. His own theory is salvageable, therefore, in a way that Cratylus' is not.

§13 Socrates on the Correctness of Names

The dialectical examination of Hermogenes and Cratylus has brought their views closer together; each has had to make some

---

23. See my "Motion, Rest, and Dialectic in the Sophist," *Archiv für Geschichte der Philosophie* 67 (1985), 47–64.

24. See M. M. A. Mackenzie, "Putting the *Cratylus* in Its Place," *Classical Quarterly* 36 (1986), 124–50. David Sedley has pointed out to me in correspondence that Plato's use of the future participle '*gnosomenou*' at 440a1 implies that he is thinking of the form as changing *before* one can get to know it. If he is right, Plato may not be anticipating the *Sophist* here at all.

concessions to the other's theory. But any final synthesis of their views remains implicit in Socrates' own scattered views. Nonetheless, such a synthesis is strongly hinted at. Following up hints is a risky business of course, and there is a greater likelihood of going off the tracks, but we would be poor readers of Plato if we insisted on always playing safe.

A successful name-giver must, as we saw (§9), perform two tasks. First, he must *construct* names that express the natures of things; he must be a name-maker. Second, he must *assign* names to things correctly, that is to say, no name must be assigned to a thing unless it expresses its nature; he must be a rule-setter.

To construct names successfully, the name-giver must have prior, non-name-mediated knowledge of the forms that the natures of things resemble (§4). For example, he must know that justice is a structure that exists in a soul if and only if its rational part rules its appetitive part with the help of the spirited part (*Republic* 443c–444a). We may abbreviate this to:

$$\text{Justice} = {}^{*}[R + S \cdot A]$$

This is a definition of a real, non-linguistic entity. But while knowing the definitions of all the forms and natures is necessary to being a good name-maker, it isn't sufficient. For one could know these definitions and yet not know how to express them correctly in a name. That is why the name-maker must also have non-name-mediated knowledge of the form of a name (389d6–7).

An example will help us understand what this latter knowledge contributes to name-making. Let us suppose that

$$^{*}, R, S, A, [,], \cdot$$

are first principles, elements that cannot be defined in the way that justice can. They are thus things which, if correctly named, must be given *primary* names. Knowing the form of a (primary) name will enable the name-giver to grasp its being or essence by giving it a name whose letters or syllables imitate or naturally resemble it (424a9–b2). For simplicity's sake, we may construct these names by following our usual convention of enclosing them in single quotes. Thus '*' is the name of *, and so on. Knowing the form of a (derivative) name will then enable the name-giver to assemble primary names into correct derivative ones. In other words, it will enable him to know such things as this:

$$\text{'Justice'} = \text{' '*'^'['^'R'^'+'^'S'^'•'^'A'^']' '}$$

(where '^' means 'is followed by'). This is a definition of a name —'justice'—in terms of other names.

Knowledge of these name-definitions comes to the name-maker from the dialectician, who "knows how to ask and answer questions" (390c10–11). For he is the one who uses names for their defining purpose, namely, to instruct, and so knows which ones perform well in actual use. Consequently, names defined as he proposes will not suffer the ignominious fate of the Heraclitean definitions scrutinized earlier: *their* analyses will not reveal the name-giver to have contradicted himself (438c5–6) or land him in unstable *aporia*. If other dialogues are to be our guide, it is also the dialectician who, using knowledge provided by the various sciences, constructs the definitions of the various forms (*Euthydemus* 290c, *Republic* 510c–511e). Just how he does this, however, and how doing it differs, if it does, from that of constructing dialectically defensible name-definitions need not concern us.[25]

In the ideal case, all these names, primary and derivative, will express natures exactly (435c1–d1). But they do not have to meet this very exacting condition in order to be naturally correct names. It is enough, as we know, if they include the pattern of those natures. But what exactly is the pattern of a nature? Socrates does not tell us and it is hard to know for sure. Nonetheless, educated guesses are possible. The generic form of a shuttle is less specific than the specific form of a particular sort of shuttle. The nature that gets embodied in a particular piece of wood by a shuttle-maker who is copying the specific form may include some extraneous features, just as '*bêta*' includes extraneous letters beyond the '*b*' it names (393d6–e8). As long as the features that appear in the definition of the generic form of shuttle get embodied in the wood, however, the thing is a shuttle. By

---

25. See my *Philosopher-Kings*, 71–79.

the same token, as long as the features that appear in the definition of the name 'shuttle' appear in the name, it will express the
pattern of the nature of a specific shuttle and be a naturally correct (even if not fully correct) name of it. On this account, patterns are generic forms.[26]

Like Hermogenes', our understanding of this entire account
of correct names would be immeasurably enhanced if we could
be shown some genuine elementary names together with their
elemental nominata and some genuine derivative ones (391a1–3).
But that is clearly impossible. It is important to remember, therefore, that Socrates' own examples are hypothetical, they presuppose Heracliteanism, and, in one important respect at least,
somewhat misleading. Socrates is explicit, after all, that primary
names imitate forms or natures, and that natures are to be con-
trasted with sensory qualities, such as colors and sounds
(423c11–424a1). Strictly speaking, therefore, he cannot think that
primary names naturally imitate forms by, say, sounding like
them. Moreover, forms, even forms of sensory qualities, are
intelligible or abstract entities, not sensory ones (*Republic*
507a–511e). Hence, whatever the nature of the natural resemblance relation is that holds between primary names and the
forms they name, it too must be intelligible or abstract, more like
the one, whatever it is, that holds between the recursively defined numerals and the natural numbers than the onomatopoeic
one that holds, say, between 'rugged' and ruggedness. Given
that correct names can exist in languages that sound very different from one another and have different alphabets ('*dog*' neither
looks nor sounds like '*KUΩN*'), that is the result we ought, in
any case, to expect (390a4–7).[27]

---

26. See my "Platonic Politics and the Good," *Political Theory* 23 (1995),
411–424.
27. The problem of the identity of names is genuinely difficult, precisely because the same name can be represented in very different
graphic or phonetic systems (consider Morse code, binary, American
Sign Language, and semaphore, for examples) and then be pronounced
or written in many different ways by individual users of those systems
(no two speakers make exactly the same sounds in uttering 'dog', or
make exactly the same marks in writing it). It is no easy matter, therefore, to identify the type name of which 'dog' is a token.

It may well be, however, that Socrates intends the case of numerals to cast doubt on the existence of any natural resemblance relationship between primary names and the forms they name. Let us look again at what he says:

> Even though the name I utter is unlike the thing I mean—since '*l*' is unlike hardness (to revert to your example). But if that's right, surely you have entered into a convention with yourself, and the correctness of names has become a matter of convention for you, for isn't it the chance of usage and convention that makes both like and unlike letters express things? And even if usage is completely different from convention, still you must say that expressing something isn't a matter of likeness but of usage, since usage, it seems, enables both like and unlike names to express things. Since we agree on these points, Cratylus, for I take your silence as a sign of agreement, both convention and usage must contribute something to expressing what we mean when we speak. Consider numbers, Cratylus, since you want to have recourse to them. Where do you think you'll get names that are like each one of the numbers, if you don't allow this agreement and convention of yours to have some control over the correctness of names? (435a5–c2)

The opening sentences certainly make it seem that letters that are either like or unlike a form or nature can be what make a primary name containing them into a name of that nature, and that it is convention or usage that makes this possible. On this account, natural correctness appears only at the level of derivative names. In the case we imagined earlier, for example, the name-maker establishes a convention assigning '*' to *, which is not based on any natural resemblance relation between them. But

$$\text{' '}\mathbf{*'^{\wedge}'['^{\wedge}'R'^{\wedge}'+'^{\wedge}'S'^{\wedge}'\bullet'^{\wedge}'A'^{\wedge}']' \text{ '}$$

is still a naturally correct name for justice. If we understand Socrates' point in this way, the name-maker uses convention twice. Once in assigning primary names to forms of the requisite type, and again, in the way that we are about to describe, in assigning names to things other than forms.

Through his association with the dialectician, the name-maker has completed the first of his tasks: he has made naturally correct names for all the forms. It remains for him to carry out the other part of his task and assign those names correctly to things. He must ensure that the name of a form is assigned only to things which have a nature that imitates it. This he does by setting rules or conventions governing the use of names. That is why the name-giver is a rule-setter (388e7–389a3), and why Socrates says that it is rules or conventions that provide us with the names we use (388d9–14).

In Socrates' view, then, there is a place—indeed, more than one place—for convention in the correctness of names, as Hermogenes argued. His theory is therefore a true synthesis of the opposed theories of his interlocutors.[28]

§14 Conclusion

The ideal described in the *Cratylus* is of an origin for language in genuine, non-name-mediated knowledge of the natures of things. This is not, obviously, a humanly achievable ideal. We see the world through a linguistic lens ground according to old recipes reflecting the interests and powers of all those whose use and abuse of language has helped to make the lens what it is. The idea of starting anew, without our linguistic and conceptual inheritance from the past, is a fantasy, not a real possibility. It is crucial, therefore, to see that the ideal *described* in the *Cratylus* is not the one *dramatized* in it. For in the dialogue there are no contemplators of unmediated being, only dialectical investigators, so to speak, of the verb 'to be'.

Nowhere is this more true than in the closing lines. Socrates, as we saw, recognizes the necessity for human beings to "keep re-investigating" their views (428d2–4). "The unexamined life," as he puts it more famously elsewhere, "is not the life for a human being" (*Apology* 38a5–6). When Cratylus is leaving, Socrates exhorts him to continue his search for truth:

---

28. I have benefited in writing this section from Allan Silverman's excellent paper, "Plato's *Cratylus*: The Naming of Nature and the Nature of Naming," *Oxford Studies in Ancient Philosophy* 10 (1992), 25–71.

It's certainly possible that things are that [Heraclitean] way, Cratylus, but it is also possible that they are not. So you must investigate them courageously and thoroughly and not accept anything easily—you are still young and in your prime, after all. Then after you've investigated them, if you happen to discover the truth, you can share it with me. (440d1–6)

Cratylus' reply makes it clear that this exhortation falls on deaf ears:

I'll do that. But I assure you, Socrates, that I have already investigated them and have taken a lot of trouble over the matter, and things seem to me to be very much more as Heraclitus says they are. (440d7–e2)

These are almost his final words. Having uttered them, he is seen on his way (*propempein*) by Hermogenes. Cratylus is thus as wrong about the correctness of Hermogenes' name as he is about things and names. For Hermogenes *is* acting like a true son of Hermes *pompaios*, who sees souls on their way to Hades.[29] But it is Cratylus' refusal to reexamine his own views that condemns him in the end to the silence of the dead.

---

29. I am grateful to Rachel Barney for this nice point.

CRATYLUS[1]

[OR ON THE CORRECTNESS OF NAMES]

HERMOGENES: Shall we let Socrates here join our discussion?   383a

CRATYLUS: If you like.

HERMOGENES: Cratylus[2] says, Socrates, that there is a correctness of name for each thing, one that belongs to it by nature. A thing's name isn't whatever people agree to call it—some bit of their native language that applies to it—but there is a natural correctness of names, which is the same for everyone, Greek or foreigner. So, I ask him whether his own name is truly 'Craty-   b
lus'. He agrees that it is. "What about Socrates?" I say. "His name is 'Socrates'," he says. "Does this also hold for everyone else? Is the name we call him his name?" "It certainly doesn't hold of you. Your name isn't 'Hermogenes', not even if everyone calls you by it." Eagerly, I ask him to tell me what he means. He responds sarcastically and makes nothing clear. He pretends to   384a
possess some private knowledge which would force me to agree with him and say the very things about names that he says himself, were he to express it in plain terms. So, if you can somehow interpret Cratylus' oracular utterances, I'd gladly listen. Though I'd really rather find out what you yourself have to say about the correctness of names, if that's all right with you.

SOCRATES: Hermogenes, son of Hipponicus, there is an ancient proverb that "fine things are very difficult" to know about, and it certainly isn't easy to get to know about names. To be sure, if   b
I'd attended Prodicus' fifty-drachma lecture course,[3] which he

---

1. The translation is based on John Burnet's edition of the Greek text, though I have sometimes adopted readings from the new edition by E. A. Duke et al.
2. See Introduction, pp. xi–xii.
3. Prodicus of Ceos was a sophist and a contemporary of Socrates.

1

himself advertises as an exhaustive treatment of the topic,
there'd be nothing to prevent you from learning the precise
truth about the correctness of names straightway. But as I've
c   heard only the one-drachma course, I don't know the truth
about it. Nonetheless, I am ready to investigate it along with
you and Cratylus. As for his denying that your real name is
'Hermogenes', I suspect he's making fun of you. Perhaps, he
thinks you want to make money but fail every time you try.[4] In
any case, as I was saying, it's certainly difficult to know about
these matters, so we'll have to conduct a joint investigation to
see who is right, you or Cratylus.

HERMOGENES: Well, Socrates, I've often talked with Cratylus—
and with lots of other people, for that matter—and no one is
able to persuade me that the correctness of names is determined
d   by anything besides convention and agreement. I believe that
any name you give a thing is its correct name. If you change its
name and give it another, the new one is as correct as the old.
For example, when we give names to our domestic slaves, the
new ones are as correct as the old.[5] No name belongs to a particular thing by nature, but only because of the rules and usage of
those who establish the usage and call it by that name. However,
e   if I'm wrong about this, I'm ready to listen not just to Cratylus
but to anyone, and to learn from him too.

SOCRATES: Perhaps you're on to something, Hermogenes, let's
385a see. Are you saying that whatever anyone decides to call[6] a particular thing is its name?

HERMOGENES: I am.

SOCRATES: Whether it is a private individual or a community
that does so?

---

4. Hermes is the god of profit and "Hermogenes" means "son of Hermes." A different account of the name is given at 407e–408b.
5. Slaves with foreign names were usually given new Greek names by
their masters.
6. Reading *ho ean thê(i) kalein*.

HERMOGENES: Yes.

SOCRATES: What about this? Suppose I call one of the things that are—for instance, the one we now call 'man'—suppose I give *that* the name 'horse' and give the one we now call 'horse' the name 'man'. Will the same thing have the public name 'man' but the private name 'horse'? Is that what you mean?

HERMOGENES: Yes.[7]   *b1*

SOCRATES: So whatever each person says is the name of some-   *d*
thing, for him, that is its name?

HERMOGENES: Yes.

SOCRATES: And however many names someone says there are for each thing, it will really have that number at whatever time he says it?

HERMOGENES: Yes, Socrates, for I can't conceive of any other way in which names could be correct. I call a thing by the name I gave it; you call it by the different name you gave it. In the same way, I see that each different city[8] has different names for the same things—Greeks differing from other Greeks, and Greeks   *e*
from foreigners. *whatever name someone sees M for something is correct*

SOCRATES: Let's see, Hermogenes, whether the same also seems to you to hold of the things that are. Is the being or essence of each of them something private for each person, as Protagoras tells us? He says that man is "the measure of all things," and that things are to me as they appear to me, and are to you as   *386a*
they appear to you. Do you agree, or do you believe that things
have some fixed being or essence of their own?

different perspectives

---

7. Following Malcolm Schofield, "A Displacement in the Text of the *Cratylus," Classical Quarterly* 22 (1972), 246–53, I transfer 385b2–d1 to follow 387c5.
8. Reading *idia(i) hekastais* with Duke et al.

HERMOGENES: There have been times, Socrates, when I have been so puzzled that I've been driven to take refuge in Protagoras' doctrine, even though I really don't believe it.

b   SOCRATES: What's that? Have you actually been driven to believe that there is no such thing as a bad man?

HERMOGENES: No, by god, I haven't. Indeed, I've often found myself believing that there are *very* bad ones, and plenty of them.

SOCRATES: What? Have you never believed that there are any who are very good?

HERMOGENES: Not many. → *good men*, *many bad ones* [*not many*]

SOCRATES: But you did believe that there were *some* good ones?

HERMOGENES: I did.

SOCRATES: And what do you hold about such people? Or is it this: the very good are very wise,[9] while the very bad are very foolish?

c   HERMOGENES: Yes, that's what I believe.

SOCRATES: But if Protagoras is telling the truth—if it *is* the *Truth*[10] that things are for each person as he believes them to be, how is it possible for one person to be wise and another foolish?

HERMOGENES: It isn't possible.

SOCRATES: You strongly believe, it seems to me, that if wisdom exists, and foolishness likewise, then Protagoras cannot be

---

9. See 392c.
10. Plato is making a pun on the title of Protagoras' book. See 391c and *Theaetetus* 162a.

telling the truth. After all, if what each person believes to be true *is* true for him, no one can truly be wiser than anyone else.

d

HERMOGENES: That's right.

SOCRATES: But you also reject Euthydemus' doctrine that everything always has every attribute simultaneously.[11] For if virtue and vice always belong to everything simultaneously, it follows once again that it is impossible for some people to be good and others to be bad.

HERMOGENES: That's true.

SOCRATES: But if neither is right, if it isn't the case that everything always has every attribute simultaneously or that each thing has a being or essence privately for each person, then it is clear that things have some fixed being or essence of their own. They are not in relation to us and are not made to fluctuate by how they appear to us. They are by themselves, in relation to their own being or essence, which is theirs by nature.

e

things are as they are and are not meant to be changed by how we interperate them

HERMOGENES: I agree, Socrates.

SOCRATES: And if things are of such a nature, doesn't the same hold of actions performed in relation to them? Or don't actions constitute some one class of the things that are?

HERMOGENES: Of course they do.

SOCRATES: So an action's performance accords with the action's own nature, and not with what we believe. Suppose, for example, that we undertake to cut something, should we make the cut in whatever way *we* choose and with whatever tool *we* choose? Or, if in each case we choose to cut in accord with the nature of cutting and being cut and with the natural tool for cutting, will we succeed and cut correctly? Whereas, if we try

387a

---

11. Euthydemus was a sophist. He appears in the dialogue named after him.

to cut contrary to nature, we'll be in error and accomplish nothing? *things have a certain way they are meant to be done*

b   HERMOGENES: That's my view, at least.

SOCRATES: So, again, if we undertake to burn something, our burning mustn't accord with every belief but with the correct one—that is to say, with the one that tells us how that thing burns and is burned naturally, and what the natural tool for burning it is?

HERMOGENES: That's right.

SOCRATES: And the same holds of all other actions?

HERMOGENES: Certainly.

SOCRATES: Now isn't speaking or saying one sort of action?

HERMOGENES: Yes.

SOCRATES: Then will someone speak correctly if he speaks in whatever way he believes he should speak? Or isn't it rather the case that he will accomplish something and succeed in speaking
c   if he says things in the natural way to say them, in the natural way for them to be said, and with the natural tool for saying them? But if he speaks in any other way he will be in error and accomplish nothing? *how does one or anyone know the correct way to speak?*

c5   HERMOGENES: I believe so.[12]

385b2   SOCRATES: Tell me this. Is there something you call speaking the truth and something you call speaking a falsehood?

HERMOGENES: Indeed, there is.

SOCRATES: Then some statements are true, while others are false?

---

12. Here I insert 385b2–d1; see n. 7 above.

HERMOGENES: Certainly.

SOCRATES: And those that say of the things that are that they are, are true, while those that say of the things that are that they are not, are false?

HERMOGENES: Yes.

SOCRATES: So it is possible to say both things that are and things that are not in a statement?

HERMOGENES: Certainly.

SOCRATES: Is a whole true statement true but not its parts?   c

HERMOGENES: No, the parts are also true.

SOCRATES: Are the large parts true but not the small ones, or are all of them true?

HERMOGENES: In my view, they are all true.

SOCRATES: Is there a part of a statement that's smaller than a name?

HERMOGENES: No, it is the smallest.

SOCRATES: In a true statement, is this smallest part something that's said?

HERMOGENES: Yes.

SOCRATES: And, on your view, this part is then true.

HERMOGENES: Yes.

SOCRATES: And a part of a false statement is false?

HERMOGENES: That's right.

all of a true statement is true while only part of a false statement is false

SOCRATES: So isn't it possible to say a true or a false name, since true or false statements are possible?

d   HERMOGENES: Certainly.

387c6   SOCRATES: Now using names is a part of saying; since it is by using names that people say things.

HERMOGENES: Certainly.

SOCRATES: And if speaking or saying is a sort of action, one that is about things, isn't using names also a sort of action?

HERMOGENES: Yes.

SOCRATES: And didn't we see that actions aren't in relation to us
d   but have a special nature of their own?

HERMOGENES: We did.

SOCRATES: So if we are to be consistent with what we said previously, we cannot name things as we choose; rather, we must name them in the natural way for them to be named and with the natural tool for naming them. In that way we'll accomplish something and succeed in naming, otherwise we won't.

HERMOGENES: So it seems.

SOCRATES: Again, what one has to cut, one must cut with something?

HERMOGENES: Yes.

SOCRATES: And what one has to weave, one must weave with
e   something? And what one has to drill, one must drill with something?

HERMOGENES: Certainly.

everything, every action, has a
certain way in which it is to be
done (naturally)

SOCRATES: And what one has to name, one must name with something?

HERMOGENES: That's right.

SOCRATES: What must drilling be done with?

HERMOGENES: A drill.

SOCRATES: Weaving?

HERMOGENES: A shuttle.

SOCRATES: And naming?

HERMOGENES: A name.

SOCRATES: Well done! So a name is also a sort of tool?

names are tools

HERMOGENES: That's right.

SOCRATES: And suppose I ask, "What sort of tool is a shuttle?" Isn't the answer, "One we weave with"?

HERMOGENES: Yes.

SOCRATES: What do we do when we weave? Don't we divide the warp and woof that are mixed together? *b*

HERMOGENES: Yes.

SOCRATES: And you'd be able to speak in the same way about drills and other tools?

HERMOGENES: Certainly.

SOCRATES: So you can speak this way about names? If a name is a tool, what do we do when we name?

HERMOGENES: I can't say.

classify, recognise, acknowledge, clarify, categorize

SOCRATES: Don't we instruct each other, that is to say,[13] divide things according to their natures?

HERMOGENES: Certainly.

SOCRATES: So just as a shuttle is a tool for dividing warp and woof, a name is a tool for giving instruction, that is to say, for di-
c   viding being.

HERMOGENES: Yes.

SOCRATES: Isn't a shuttle a weaver's tool?

HERMOGENES: Of course.

[handwritten margin note: token: particular instance of a type or an example of a kind]

SOCRATES: So a weaver will use shuttles well; and to use a shuttle well is to use it as a weaver does. By the same token an instructor will use names well; and to use a name well is to use it as an instructor does.

HERMOGENES: Yes.

SOCRATES: When a weaver uses a shuttle well, whose product is he using?

HERMOGENES: A carpenter's.

SOCRATES: Is everyone a carpenter or only those who possess the craft[14] of carpentry?

HERMOGENES: Only those who possess the craft.

d   SOCRATES: And whose product does a driller use well when he uses a drill?

---

13. 393d and 422d suggest that *kai* is epexegetic or explanatory here.
14. *Technê*: a word with the same sort of connotation for Socrates and Plato that 'science' has for us.

HERMOGENES: A blacksmith's.

SOCRATES: And is everyone a blacksmith or only those who possess the craft?

HERMOGENES: Only those who possess the craft.

SOCRATES: Good. So whose product does an instructor use when he uses a name?

HERMOGENES: I don't know.

SOCRATES: Can you at least tell me this? Who or what provides us with the names we use?

HERMOGENES: I don't know that either.

SOCRATES: Don't you think that rules[15] provide us with them?

what rules?

HERMOGENES: I suppose they do.

SOCRATES: So, when an instructor uses a name, he's using the product of a rule-setter.   *e*

HERMOGENES: I believe he is.

SOCRATES: Do you think that every man is a rule-setter or only the one who possesses the craft?

HERMOGENES: Only the one who possesses the craft.

how do you posses the craft of being a rule setter?

SOCRATES: It follows that it isn't every man who can give names, Hermogenes, but only a name-maker, and he, it seems, is a rule-   *389a*
setter—the kind of craftsman most rarely found among human beings.

---

15. *Nomos*: law or customary usage—itself established, as Socrates immediately goes on to say, by a *nomothetês,* usually a legislator or lawgiver, but here someone who establishes the rules of usage that give significance to names.

HERMOGENES: I suppose so.

SOCRATES: Come now, consider where a rule-setter looks in giving names. Use the previous discussion as your guide. Where does a carpenter look in making a shuttle? Isn't it to that sort of thing whose nature is to weave?

HERMOGENES: Certainly.

b   SOCRATES: Suppose the shuttle breaks while he's making it. Will he make another looking to the broken one? Or will he look to the very form to which he looked in making the one he broke?

HERMOGENES: In my view, he will look to the form.

SOCRATES: Then it would be absolutely right to call that what a shuttle itself is.[16]

HERMOGENES: I suppose so.

SOCRATES: Hence whenever he has to make a shuttle for weaving garments of any sort, whether light or heavy, linen or woolen, mustn't it possess the form of a shuttle? And mustn't he put into it the nature that naturally best suits it to perform its own work?

c   HERMOGENES: Yes.

SOCRATES: And the same holds of all other tools. When a craftsman discovers the type of tool that is naturally suited for a given type of work, he must embody it in the material out of which he is making the tool. He mustn't make the tool in whatever way he happens to choose, but in the natural way. So it seems that a blacksmith must know how to embody in iron the type of drill naturally suited for each type of work.   *everything has a natural | right way which it is to be done*

HERMOGENES: Certainly.

_____

16. See *Republic* 507b.

SOCRATES: And a carpenter must embody in wood the type of shuttle naturally suited for each type of weaving.

HERMOGENES: That's right.

SOCRATES: Because it seems that there's a type of shuttle that's naturally suited to each type of weaving. And the same holds of   *d* tools in general.

HERMOGENES: Yes.

SOCRATES: So mustn't our rule-setter also know how to embody in sounds and syllables the name naturally suited to each thing? And if he is to be an authentic giver of names, mustn't he, in making and giving each name, look to what a name itself is? And if different rule-setters do not make each name out of the same syllables, we mustn't forget[17] that different blacksmiths,   *e* who are making the same tool for the same type of work, don't all make it out of the same iron. But as long as they give it the same form—even if that form is embodied in different iron—the tool will be correct, whether it is made in Greece or abroad. Isn't   *390a* that so? *names can be different (languages) but if forms are the same it is correct (meaning)*

HERMOGENES: Certainly.

SOCRATES: Don't you evaluate Greek and foreign rule-setters in the same way? Provided they give each thing the form of name suited to it, no matter what syllables it is embodied in, they are equally good rule-setters, whether they are in Greece or abroad.

names suit things, language doesn't matter

HERMOGENES: Certainly.

SOCRATES: Now, who is likely to know whether the appropriate form of shuttle is present in any given bit of wood? A carpenter   *b* who makes it or a weaver who uses it?[18]

---

17. Reading *agnoein* with the mss.
18. See *Republic* 601c ff.

Knows if it is correct!
makes it < uses it

HERMOGENES: In all likelihood, Socrates, it is the one who uses it.

SOCRATES: So who uses what a lyre-maker produces? Isn't he the one who would know best how to supervise the manufacture of lyres and would also know whether what has been made has been well made or not?

HERMOGENES: Certainly.

SOCRATES: Who is that?

HERMOGENES: A lyre-player.

SOCRATES: And who will supervise a ship-builder?

c HERMOGENES: A ship's captain.

SOCRATES: And who can best supervise the work of a rule-setter, whether here or abroad, and judge its products? Isn't it whoever will use them?

HERMOGENES: Yes.

SOCRATES: And isn't that the person who knows how to ask questions?

HERMOGENES: Certainly.

SOCRATES: And he also knows how to answer them?

HERMOGENES: Yes.

SOCRATES: And what would you call someone who knows how to ask and answer questions? Wouldn't you call him a dialectician?

HERMOGENES: Yes, I would.

d SOCRATES: So it's the work of a carpenter to make a rudder. And if the rudder is to be a fine one, a ship-captain must supervise him.

HERMOGENES: Evidently.

SOCRATES: But it's the work of a rule-setter, it seems, to make a name. And if names are to be given well, a dialectician must supervise him.[19] *someone must ask questions about the name*

HERMOGENES: That's right.

SOCRATES: It follows that the giving of names can't be as inconsequential a matter as you think, Hermogenes, nor can it be the work of an inconsequential or chance person. So Cratylus is right in saying that things have natural names and that not everyone is a craftsman of names, but only someone who looks to the natural name of each thing and is able to put its form into letters and syllables.

e

8/31

HERMOGENES: I don't know how to oppose you, Socrates. It isn't easy for me suddenly to change my opinion, though. I think you would be more likely to persuade me if you showed me just what this natural correctness of names you're talking about consists in.

391a

SOCRATES: My dear Hermogenes, I don't have a position on this. You have forgotten what I told you a while ago, namely that I didn't know about names but that I would investigate them with you. And now that we *are* investigating them, you and I, at least this much is clearer than before, that names do possess some sort of natural correctness and that it isn't every man who knows how to name things well. Isn't that right?

b

HERMOGENES: Certainly.

SOCRATES: So our next task is to try to discover what this correctness is, if indeed you want to know.

HERMOGENES: Of course I do.

SOCRATES: Then investigate the matter.

---

19. See *Republic* 532a ff.

HERMOGENES: How am I to do that?

SOCRATES: The most correct way is together with people who already know, but you must pay them well and show gratitude besides[20]—these are the sophists. Your brother Callias got his reputation for wisdom from them in return for a lot of money. So you had better beg and implore him to teach you what he learned from Protagoras about the correctness of names, since you haven't yet come into any money of your own.

HERMOGENES: But it would be absurd for me to beg for Protagoras' "Truth," Socrates, as if I desired the things contained in it and thought them worthwhile, when I totally reject them.[21]

SOCRATES: Well, if that doesn't suit you, you'll have to learn from Homer and the other poets.

HERMOGENES: What does Homer say about names, Socrates, and where does he say it?

SOCRATES: In lots of places. The best and most important are the ones in which he distinguishes between the names humans call things and those the gods call them. Or don't you think that these passages tell us something remarkable about the correctness of names? Surely, the gods call things by their naturally correct names—or don't you think so?

HERMOGENES: I certainly know that if they call them by any names at all, it's by the correct ones. But what passages are you referring to?

SOCRATES: Do you know where he says that the Trojan river that had single combat with Hephaestus is "called 'Xanthos' by the gods and 'Skamandros' by men"?[22]

20. Cf. *Apology* 20a1–2, *Theages* 128a7.
21. See 386c.
22. Homer, *Iliad* 21.342–80 and 20.74.

HERMOGENES: I certainly do.

SOCRATES: And don't you think it's an awe-inspiring thing to know that the river is more correctly called *'Xanthos'* than *'Ska-*   *392a* *mandros'*? Or consider, if you like, when he says about a certain bird that

> How do they know what the Gods call it?
> *The gods call it* 'chalkis' *but men call it* 'kumindis'.[23]

Do you think it's an inconsequential matter to learn that it is far more correct to call this bird *'chalkis'* than to call it *'kumindis'*? What about all the similar things that Homer and the other poets tell us? For example, that it is more correct to call a certain hill *'Murinê'* than *'Batieia'*?[24] But perhaps these examples are too   *b* hard for you and me to figure out. It is easier and more within human power, I think, to investigate the kind of correctness Homer ascribes to 'Skamandrios' and 'Astyanax', which he says are the names of Hector's son. You know, of course, the lines where you'll find what I'm talking about.

HERMOGENES: Certainly.

SOCRATES: Which of the names given to the boy do you suppose Homer thought was more correct, 'Astyanax' or 'Skamandrios'?

HERMOGENES: I really can't say.   *c*

SOCRATES: Look at it this way. If you were asked who gives names more correctly, those who are wiser or those who are more foolish,[25] what would you answer?

HERMOGENES: That it is clearly those who are wiser.

---

23. *Iliad* 14.291.
24. *Iliad* 2.813 ff.
25. See 386b.

SOCRATES: And which class do you think is wiser on the whole, a city's women or its men?[26]

HERMOGENES: Its men. *sexist!!!*

SOCRATES: Now you know, don't you, that Homer tells us that
d   Hector's son was called 'Astyanax' by the men of Troy? But if the men called him 'Astyanax', isn't it clear that 'Skamandrios' must be what the women called him?

HERMOGENES: Probably so.   *gods name (wise)*   *men name (foolish)*

SOCRATES: And didn't Homer also think that the Trojans were wiser than their women?

HERMOGENES: I suppose he did.

SOCRATES: So mustn't he have thought that 'Astyanax' was a more correct name for the boy than 'Skamandrios'?

HERMOGENES: Evidently.

SOCRATES: Well, let's investigate why it is more correct. Doesn't Homer himself suggest a very good explanation when he says

e   *He alone defended their city and long walls?*[27]

For because of this, you see, it seems correct to call the son of the defender 'Astyanax' or lord-of-a-city (*astu anax*) which, as Homer says, his father was defending.

name has higher honor b/c given by gods?

HERMOGENES: That seems right to me.

SOCRATES: It does? I don't understand it yet myself, Hermogenes, but you do?

---

26. Cf. *Republic* 455c–d.
27. *Iliad* 22.507. Hector is being referred to.

HERMOGENES: I certainly do not.

SOCRATES: But, my good friend, didn't Homer also give Hector
his name?   *393a*

HERMOGENES: What if he did?

SOCRATES: Well, it seems to me that 'Hector' is more or less the
same as 'Astyanax', since both names[28] seem to be Greek. After
all, 'lord' (*'anax'*) and 'possessor' (*'hektôr'*)[29] signify pretty much
the same, since both are names for a king. Surely, a man possesses that of which he is lord, since it is clear that he controls,
owns, and has it. But perhaps you think I'm talking nonsense,   *b*
and that I'm wrong to suppose that I've found a clue to Homer's
beliefs about the correctness of names.

HERMOGENES: No, I don't think you're wrong. You may well
have found a clue.

SOCRATES: At any rate, it seems to me that it is right to call a
lion's offspring a 'lion' and a horse's offspring a 'horse'. I'm not
talking about some monster other than a horse that happens to
be born from a horse but one that is a natural offspring of its
kind. If, contrary to nature, a horse gave birth to a calf, it should   *c*
be called a 'calf', not a 'colt'. And if something that isn't a
human offspring is born to a human, I don't think it should be
called a 'human'. And the same applies to trees and all the rest.
Don't you agree? passing down names

HERMOGENES: I agree.

SOCRATES: Good. But you had better watch out in case I trick
you, for by the same argument any offspring of a king should be
called a 'king'. But it doesn't matter whether the same thing is
signified by the same syllables or by different ones. And if a let-   *d*
ter is added or subtracted, that doesn't matter either, so long as

---

28. Reading *ta onomata* with Duke et al.
29. From the verb *echein* ('to have').

the being or essence of the thing is in control and is expressed in its name.

HERMOGENES: How do you mean?

SOCRATES: It's something fairly simple. You know that when we speak of the elements or letters of the alphabet, it is their names we utter, not the letters themselves, except in the case of these four, *e*, *u*, *o*, and *ô*.[30] We make names for all the other vowels and
e   consonants, as you know, by uttering additional letters together with them. But as long as we include the force or power of the letter, we may correctly call it by that name, and it will express it for us. Take '*bêta*', for example. The addition of '*ê*', '*t*', and '*a*' does no harm and doesn't prevent the whole name from expressing the nature of that element or letter which the rule-setter wished to name, so well did he know how to give names to the letters.

HERMOGENES: I believe you're right.

SOCRATES: Doesn't the same argument apply to 'king'? For a
394a   king will probably be the son of a king, a good man the son of a good man, a fine man the son of a fine one, and so on.[31] So, unless a monster is born, the offspring of a kind will be of the same kind and should be called by the same name. But because of variation there is in their syllables, names that are really the same seem different to the uninitiated. Similarly, a doctor's medicines, which have different colors and perfumes added to them, appear different to us, although they are really the same
b   and appear the same to a doctor, who looks only to their power to cure and isn't disconcerted by the additives. Similarly, someone who knows about names looks to their force or power and isn't disconcerted if a letter is added, transposed, or subtracted, or even if the force a name possesses is embodied in different

---

30. The names 'epsilon', 'upsilon', 'omicron', and 'omega' were not used in Plato's time; one simply pronounced the sound.
31. See *Republic* 415a ff.

letters altogether. So, for example, in the names 'Hector' and 'Astyanax', which we were discussing just now, none of the letters is the same, except 't', but they signify the same anyway. And what letters does 'Archepolis'—'Ruler-of-a-city'—have in   c
common with them? Yet, it expresses the same thing. Many other names signify simply king; others signify general, for example, 'Agis' ('Leader'), 'Polemarchus' ('War-lord'), 'Eupolemus' ('Good-warrior'); and still others signify doctor, for example, 'Iatrocles' ('Famous-healer') and 'Acesimbrotus' ('Healer-of-mortals'). And we might perhaps find many others, which differ in their letters and syllables, but which have the same force or power when spoken. Is that plain to you or not?

HERMOGENES: Certainly.   d

SOCRATES: Then those that are born according to nature should be given the same names as their fathers.

HERMOGENES: Yes.

SOCRATES: What about the ones that are born contrary to nature, those that are some form of monster? For instance, when a good and pious man has an impious son, the latter shouldn't have his father's name but that of the kind to which he belongs, just as in our earlier example of a horse having a calf as offspring?[32]

HERMOGENES: Yes.

SOCRATES: Therefore the impious son of a pious father should be   e
given the name of the kind to which he belongs.

HERMOGENES: That's right.

SOCRATES: Then he shouldn't be called 'Theophilus' ('God-beloved') or 'Mnesitheus' ('Mindful-of-god'), or anything of that sort, but something that signifies the opposite, if indeed names are to be actually correct.

name must fit traits ?

32. See 393b–c, and Aristotle, *Generation of Animals* 767b5 ff.

HERMOGENES: That's absolutely right, Socrates.

SOCRATES: Thus the name 'Orestes' ('Mountain-man') is surely correct, Hermogenes, whether it was given to him by chance or by some poet, who displayed in his name the brutality, savagery, and ruggedness of his nature.[33]

395a HERMOGENES: It seems so, Socrates.

SOCRATES: And his father's name also seems to accord with nature.

HERMOGENES: It does.

SOCRATES: Yes, for Agamemnon is someone who worked hard and persevered, bringing his plans to completion because of his virtue or excellence. The stay of his army[34] in Troy and his perseverance there is a sign of this. And thus the name 'Agamemnon' signifies that this man is admirable (*agastos*) for holding his

b ground (*epimonê*). The name 'Atreus' also seems to be correct; for both his murder of Chrysippus and his cruelty to Thyestes were damaging and destructive (*atêra*) to his virtue. However, the meaning of his name is somewhat distorted and obscure, so that it doesn't express his nature to everyone. But to those who understand about names it adequately expresses what 'Atreus' means. For whether the name accords with his stubbornness (*ateires*), or his boldness (*atrestos*), or his destructiveness (*atêros*),

c it is correctly given to him. I think Pelops also has a fitting name; for 'Pelops' signifies he who sees only what is near at hand (*pelas, opsis*).

HERMOGENES: How is that?

SOCRATES: Because, according to legend, he didn't think about or foresee what the long-term consequences of murdering Myrtilus would be for his entire family, or all the misery that would

---

33. '*Oros*' means mountain.
34. Reading *plêthous* with Duke et al.

overwhelm them. In his eagerness to win Hippodameia by any available means, he saw only what was ready to hand and on the spot—that is to say, what was nearby (*pelas*). Everyone   *d* would agree, too, that 'Tantalus' was given correctly and according to nature, if what's said about its bearer is true.

HERMOGENES: What's that?

SOCRATES: They say that many terrible misfortunes happened to him in his life—the last of which was the total overthrow of his country—and that, in Hades, after his death, he had a stone suspended (*talanteia*) over his head, in wondrous harmony with his name. It's exactly as if someone had wished to name him 'Talan-   *e* tatos' ('Most-weighed-upon') but had disguised the name and said 'Tantalus' instead. In some such way, in any case, the chance of legend supplied him with this name. His father, who is said to have been Zeus, also seems to have had an altogether fine name given to him—but it isn't easy to figure out. That's be-   *396a* cause the name 'Zeus' is exactly like a phrase that we divide into two parts, 'Zêna' and 'Dia', some of us using one of them and some the other.[35] But these two names, reunited into one, express the nature of the god—which is just what we said a name should do. Certainly, no one is more the cause of life (*zên*), whether for us or for anything else, than the ruler and king of all things. Thus 'Zêna' and 'Dia' together correctly name the god that is always the cause of life (*di' hon zên*) for all creatures. But,   *b* as I say, his name, which is really one, is divided in two, 'Dia' and 'Zêna'. When one hears that Zeus is the son of Kronos, one might find that offensive at first, and it might seem more reasonable to say that he is the offspring of a great intellect. But in fact Kronos' name signifies not a child (*koros*), but the purity and clarity of his intellect or understanding.[36] According to legend, he was the son of Ouranos (Heaven), whose name is also cor-

---

35. 'Zeus' (nominative) has two declensions, one of which (a poetical one) has 'Zêna' in the accusative, the other (the ordinary one) has 'Dia'.
36. Socrates is treating Kronos' name as deriving not from 'koros' but from 'korein' ('to sweep'). Kronos' character is spotless and his intelligence clear because both have been well swept.

rectly given, for the sight of what is above is well called by the
name *'ourania'* ('heavenly')—looking at the things above (*horôsa*
c   *ta anô*)—and astronomers say, Hermogenes, that that results in
purity of intellect.[37] If I could remember Hesiod's genealogy,
and the even earlier ancestors of the gods he mentions, I
wouldn't have stopped explaining the correctness of the names
he gives them, until I had tested this wisdom which has suddenly come upon me—I do not know from where—to see
d   whether or not it holds up till the end.

HERMOGENES: Indeed, Socrates, you do seem to me to be exactly
like a prophet who has suddenly been inspired to deliver oracles.

SOCRATES: Yes, Hermogenes, and I, for my part, mostly blame
Euthyphro, of the deme of Prospalta,[38] for its coming upon me. I
was with him at dawn, lending an ear to his lengthy discussion.
He must have been inspired, because it looks as though he has
not only filled my ears with his superhuman wisdom[39] but taken
possession of my soul as well. So it seems to me that this is what
e   we ought to do: Today, we'll use this wisdom and finish our examination of names, but tomorrow, if the rest of you agree, we'll
exorcise it and purify ourselves, as soon as we've found someone—whether priest or wise man—who is clever at that kind of
397a   purification.

HERMOGENES: That's fine with me. I'd be very glad to hear what
remains to be said about names.

SOCRATES: Then that's what we must do. Since we now have
some sort of outline to follow, which names do you want us to
begin with, in order to find out whether names themselves will
testify to us that they are not given by chance, but have some
b   sort of correctness? The names that heroes and men are said to

---

37. See *Republic* 528e ff.
38. Probably the Euthyphro who appears in the dialogue of that name,
where he is described as claiming authority on Ouranos, Kronos, and
Zeus.
39. See *Apology* 20d.

have might perhaps deceive us. After all, as we saw at the beginning, they are often given because they are the names of ancestors, and some of them are wholly inappropriate. Many, too,
are given in the hope that they will prove appropriate, such as
'Eutychides' ('Son-of-good-fortune'), 'Sosias' ('Savior'), 'Theophilus' ('God-beloved'), and many others. In my view, we must
leave such names aside. We are most likely to find correctly
given names among those concerned with the things that by nature always are, since it is proper for their names to be given
with the greatest care, and some may even be the work of a more   *c*
than human power.

HERMOGENES: I think that's sensible, Socrates.

SOCRATES: So isn't it right to begin by seeing why the name
'theoi' ('gods') is itself one that the gods are correctly called?

HERMOGENES: It probably is.

SOCRATES: I suspect something like this. It seems to me that the
first inhabitants of Greece believed only in those gods in which
many foreigners still believe today—the sun, moon, earth, stars,   *d*
and sky. And, seeing that these were always moving or running,
they gave them the name *'theoi'* because it was their nature to
run (*thein*). Later, when they learned about the other gods, they
called them all by that name. Does that seem likely—or am I
talking nonsense?

HERMOGENES: It's very likely.

SOCRATES: What shall we investigate next? Clearly, it's daimons,[40] then heroes, then humans, isn't it?

HERMOGENES: Yes, daimons are next.[41]

---

40. Daimons are gods or children of the gods (*Apology* 27d–e), and
messengers from the gods (*Symposium* 202e).
41. Reading *ê dêlon dê hoti daimonas te kai hêrôas kai anthrôpous daimonas*,
attributing *ê dêlon . . . anthrôpous* to Socrates and *daimonas* to Hermogenes.

e SOCRATES: And what is the correct meaning of the name 'daimons', Hermogenes? See if you think there's anything in what
I'm about to say.

HERMOGENES: Say it, and I will.

SOCRATES: Do you know what Hesiod says daimons are?

HERMOGENES: No, I don't remember.

SOCRATES: Do you remember that he speaks of a golden race,
which was the first race of human beings to be born?

HERMOGENES: Yes, I remember that.

SOCRATES: He says this about it:

398a

> *Since this race has been eclipsed by fate,*
> *They are called sacred daimons;*
> *They live on earth and are good,*
> *Warding off evil and guarding mortal men.*[42]

HERMOGENES: So what?

SOCRATES: Well, I don't think he's saying that the golden race is
by nature made of gold, but that it is good and fine. I consider it
a proof of this that he calls us a race of iron.

HERMOGENES: That's true.

SOCRATES: So don't you think that if someone who presently exists were good, Hesiod would say that he too belonged to the
b golden race?

HERMOGENES: He probably would.

SOCRATES: Are good people any different from wise ones?

---

42. *Works and Days*, 121–3, with minor variations.

HERMOGENES: No, they aren't.

SOCRATES: It is principally because daimons are wise and knowing (*daêmones*), I think, that Hesiod says they are named 'daimons' (*'daimones'*). In our older Attic dialect, we actually find the word *'daêmones'*. So, Hesiod and many other poets speak well when they say that when a good man dies, he has a great destiny and a great honor and becomes a 'daimon', which is a name given to him because it accords with wisdom.[43] And I myself assert, indeed, that every good man, whether alive or dead, is daimonic, and is correctly called a 'daimon'.[44]

c

HERMOGENES: And I think that I completely agree with you, Socrates. But what about the name 'hero' (*'hêrôs'*)? What is it?

SOCRATES: That one isn't so hard to understand because the name has been little altered. It expresses the fact that heroes were born out of love (*erôs*).

HERMOGENES: How do you mean?

SOCRATES: Don't you know that the heroes are demigods?

god + human

HERMOGENES: So what?

SOCRATES: So all of them sprang from the love of a god for a mortal woman or of a mortal man for a goddess. And if, as before, you investigate the matter by relying on old Attic, you will get a better understanding, since it will show you that the name 'hero' (*'hêrôs'*) is only a slightly altered form of the word love (*'erôs'*)—the very thing from which the heroes sprang. And either this is the reason they were called 'heroes' or else because they were sophists, clever speech-makers (*rhêtores*) and dialecticians, skilled questioners (*erôtan*)—for *'eirein'* is the same as *'legein'* ('to speak'). And therefore, as we were saying just now, in

d

---

43. Since good men are wise and knowing (386b), the name 'daimon' appropriately expresses their natures.
44. See *Republic* 540b.

the Attic dialect, the heroes turn out to be speech-makers and
e   questioners. Hence the noble breed of heroes turns out be a race
of speech-makers and sophists. That isn't hard to understand.
But can you tell me why members of the human race are called
'humans' (*'anthrôpoi'*)? That's much harder to understand.

HERMOGENES: How could *I* do that, Socrates? I wouldn't strain
myself to find it even if I could, because I think you're much
more likely to find it than I am.

SOCRATES: You really do have faith in Euthyphro's inspiration, it
399a   seems.

HERMOGENES: Clearly.

SOCRATES: And you're certainly right to have faith in it. Indeed,
I seem to have had such a clever insight just now, that, if I'm not
careful, I'll be in danger of becoming altogether *too* wise before
the day is out. So pay attention. First of all, we must bear in
mind the following point about names: we often add letters or
take them out and change the accents as well, thus swerving
aside from what we want to name. For instance, take *'Dii philos'*
('Friend-to-Zeus'). In order for us to have a name instead of a
b   phrase, we took out the second *'i'*, and pronounced the second
syllable with a grave accent instead of an acute (*'Diphilos'*). In
other cases, we do the opposite, inserting letters and pronouncing a syllable with an acute accent instead of a grave.

HERMOGENES: That's true.

SOCRATES: Now, I think our name for human beings is a case of
just this sort. It was a phrase but became a name. One letter—
'a'—has been taken away and the accent on the final syllable has
become a grave.

HERMOGENES: What do you mean?

c   SOCRATES: This. The name 'human' signifies that the other animals do not investigate or reason about anything they see, nor
do they observe anything closely. But a human being no sooner

sees something—that is to say, *'opôpe'*—than he observes it
closely and reasons about it. Hence human beings alone among
the animals are correctly named *'anthrôpos'*—one who observes
closely what he has seen (*anathrôn ha opôpe*). humans named for
observation

HERMOGENES: What comes next? May I tell you what I'd like to
have explained?

SOCRATES: Of course.

HERMOGENES: It seems to me to be next in order. We speak of the   *d*
body and soul of a human being.

SOCRATES: Certainly.

HERMOGENES: Then let's try to analyze their names as we did the
previous ones.

SOCRATES: Are you saying that we should investigate whether
soul and then body are reasonably named?

HERMOGENES: Yes.

SOCRATES: Speaking off the top of my head, I think that those
who gave soul its name had something like this in mind. They
thought that when the soul is present in the body, it causes it to
live and gives it the power to breathe the air and be revitalized
(*anapsuchon*), and that when this revitalization fails, the body
dies and is finished. It's for this reason, I think, that they called it
'soul' (*'psuchê'*). But hold on a minute, if you don't mind, for I
imagine that the followers of Euthyphro would despise this
analysis and think it crude. But I think I glimpse one they will   *400a*
find more persuasive. Have a look and see whether it pleases
you.

why soul got its name

HERMOGENES: Tell it to me and I will.

SOCRATES: When you consider the nature of every body, what,
besides the soul, do you think sustains and supports it, so that it
lives and moves about?

HERMOGENES: There isn't anything.

[handwritten: nothing besides the soul supports humans/gives them life]

SOCRATES: What about when you consider the nature of everything else? Don't you agree with Anaxagoras[45] that it is ordered and sustained by mind or soul?

HERMOGENES: I do.

b   SOCRATES: So a fine name to give this power, which supports and sustains (*ochei kai echei*) the whole of nature (*phusis*), would be 'nature-sustainer' ('*phusechê*'). This may also be pronounced more elegantly, '*psuchê*'.

HERMOGENES: Absolutely, and I also think this *is* a more scientific explanation than the other.

SOCRATES: Yes, it is. Nevertheless, it sounds funny when it's named in the true way, with its actual name (i.e., '*phusechê*').

HERMOGENES: What are we going to say about the next one?

SOCRATES: Are you referring to the name 'body'?

HERMOGENES: Yes.

SOCRATES: There's a lot to say, it seems to me—and if one distorted the name a little, there would be even more. Thus some
c   people say that the body (*sôma*) is the tomb (*sêma*) of the soul, on the grounds that it is entombed in its present life,[46] while others say that it is correctly called 'a sign' ('*sêma*') because the soul signifies whatever it wants to signify by means of the body. I think it is most likely the followers of Orpheus who gave the body its name, with the idea that the soul is being punished for something, and that the body is an enclosure or prison in which the soul is securely kept (*sôzetai*)—as the name '*sôma*' itself sug-

[handwritten margin note: 2 definitions of body]

---

45. The pre-Socratic philosopher, Anaxagoras of Clazomenae. See *Apology* 26d–e, *Phaedo* 97c–98c.
46. See *Republic* 611b ff.

gests—until the penalty is paid; for, on this view, not even a single letter of the word needs to be changed.

HERMOGENES: I think we've adequately examined these names, Socrates. But could we investigate the names of the other gods *d* along the lines of your earlier discussion of 'Zeus', to see with what kind of correctness they have been given?

SOCRATES: By Zeus, we certainly can, Hermogenes. The first and finest line of investigation, which as intelligent people we must acknowledge, is this, that we admit that we know nothing about the gods themselves or about the names they call themselves— although it is clear that they call themselves by true ones. The second best line on the correctness of names is to say, as is customary in our prayers, that we hope the gods are pleased by the names we give them, since we know no others.[47] I think this is an excellent custom. You would want us, then,[48] to begin our in-   *401a* vestigation by first announcing to the gods that we will not be investigating *them*—since we do not regard ourselves as worthy to conduct such an investigation—but rather human beings, and the beliefs they had in giving the gods their names. After all, there's no offense in doing that.

HERMOGENES: What you say seems reasonable to me, Socrates, so let's proceed as you suggest.

SOCRATES: Shall we begin, as is customary, with Hestia?[49]   *b*

HERMOGENES: All right.

SOCRATES: What do you think the person who gave Hestia her name had in mind by naming her that?

---

47. See e.g., Aeschylus, *Agamemnon*, 160–2: "Whoever Zeus may be, if this name is pleasing to him, by this name I address him."
48. Reading *boulei oun* with Duke et al.
49. Hestia, the goddess of the hearth, usually received the first part of a sacrifice and was named first in prayers and (often) in oaths.

HERMOGENES: That's no easy question to answer, in my opinion.

SOCRATES: At any rate, Hermogenes, the first name-givers weren't ordinary people, but lofty thinkers and subtle reasoners.[50]

HERMOGENES: What of it?

Hestia

SOCRATES: Well, it's obvious to me that it was people of this sort who gave things names, for even if one investigates names for-
c   eign to Attic Greek, it is equally easy to discover what they mean. In the case of what we in Attic call *'ousia'* ('being'), for ex-ample, some call it *'essia'* and others *'ôsia'*. First, then, it is rea-sonable, according to the second of these names, to call the being or essence (*ousia*) of things 'Hestia'.[51] Besides, we our-selves say that what partakes of being 'is' (*'estin'*), so being is also correctly called 'Hestia' for this reason. We even seem to have called being *'essia'* in ancient times. And, if one has sacri-fices in mind, one will realize that the name-givers themselves
d   understood matters in this way, for anyone who called the being or essence of all things *'essia'* would naturally sacrifice to Hestia before all the other gods. On the other hand, those who use the name *'ôsia'* seem to agree pretty much with Heraclitus' doctrine that the things that are are all flowing and that nothing stands fast—for the cause and originator of them is then the pusher (*ôthoun*), and so is well named *'ôsia'*. But that's enough for us to
e   say about this, since we know nothing. After Hestia, it is right to investigate Rhea and Kronos, though we've already discussed the latter's name. Now, maybe what I'm about to tell you is non-sense.[52]

HERMOGENES: Why do you say that, Socrates?

SOCRATES: Because I've got a whole swarm of wisdom in my mind!

---

50. *Meteôrologoi kai adoleschai*: These words also have some of the same negative connotations as 'airheads' and 'logic choppers'.
51. Since *'essia'* and 'Hestia' are so alike.
52. See 393a, 397c.

HERMOGENES: What sort of wisdom?

SOCRATES: It sounds completely absurd, yet it seems to me to have something very plausible about it.   *402a*

HERMOGENES: How so?

SOCRATES: I seem to see Heraclitus spouting some ancient bits of wisdom that Homer also tells us—wisdom as old as the days of Kronos and Rhea.

titans

HERMOGENES: What are you referring to?

philosopher

SOCRATES: Heraclitus says somewhere that "everything gives way and nothing stands fast", and, likening the things that are to the flowing (*rhoê*) of a river, he says that "you cannot step into the same river twice."   *b/c everythings always changing*

HERMOGENES: So he does.

SOCRATES: Well, then, don't you think that whoever gave the names 'Rhea' and 'Kronos' to the ancestors of the other gods understood things in the same way as Heraclitus? Or do you think   *b* he gave them both the names of streams (*rheumata*) merely by chance?[53] Similarly, Homer speaks of

> *Ocean, origin of the gods, and their mother Tethys;*[54]

I think Hesiod says much the same. Orpheus, too, says somewhere that

> *Fair-flowing Ocean was the first to marry,*
> *And he wedded his sister, the daughter of his mother.*[55]   *c*

---

53. 'Rhea' sounds a lot like *'rheuma'* ('stream'); apparently Socrates expects Hermogenes to hear 'Kronos' as connected with *'krounos'* ('spring').
54. *Iliad* 14.201, 302.
55. It is not clear whether Orpheus was a real person or a mythical fig-

See how they agree with each other, and how they all lean towards the doctrines of Heraclitus.

HERMOGENES: I think there's something in what you say, Socrates, but I don't understand what the name 'Tethys' means.

SOCRATES: But it practically tells you itself that it is the slightly disguised name of a spring! After all, what is strained (*diattô-*
d *menon*) and filtered (*êthoumenon*) is like a spring, and the name 'Tethys' is a compound of these two names.

HERMOGENES: That's elegant, Socrates.

SOCRATES: Indeed, it is. But what comes next? We've already talked about Zeus.

HERMOGENES: Yes, we have.

SOCRATES: So let's discuss his brothers, Poseidon and Pluto (whether we call him 'Pluto' or by his other name[56]).

Hades

HERMOGENES: Certainly.

SOCRATES: It seems to me that whoever first gave Poseidon his name, gave it to him because he saw that the force of the waves
e stopped him from walking and prevented him from going any further, just like a shackle around his feet (*desmos tôn podôn*). So he called this god, who is the ruler of the sea's power, 'Poseidon', because his 'feet were shackled' ('*posidesmon*')—the '*e*' was probably added for the sake of euphony. But perhaps this isn't what it says. Perhaps, instead of the '*s*' the name was originally pronounced with a double '*l*', because many things are known
403a (*poll' eidôs*) to the god. Or maybe he was called 'The Shaker' ('*ho seiôn*'), because he shook (*seiein*) the earth, and the '*p*' and '*d*'

---

ure. His fame in Greek myth rests on the poems in which the doctrines of Orphic religion are set forth. These are discussed in W. Burkert, *Greek Religion* (Cambridge: Harvard University Press, 1985).
56. Viz. 'Hades'.

were added on. As for Pluto, he was given that name because it accords with his being the source of wealth (*ploutos*), since wealth comes up from below the ground.[57] It seems to me that most people call him by the name 'Pluto', because they are afraid of what they can't see (*aeides*), and they assume that his other name, 'Hades', associates him with that.

HERMOGENES: And what do you think yourself, Socrates?   *b*

SOCRATES: I think people have lots of mistaken opinions about the power of this god and are unduly afraid of him. They are afraid because once we are dead we remain in his realm forever. They are terrified because the soul goes there stripped of the body. But I think that all these things, together with the name and office of the god, point in the same direction.

HERMOGENES: How so?

SOCRATES: I'll tell you how it looks to me. But first answer me   *c* this: Of the shackles that bind a living being and keep him in a place, which is stronger, force or desire?

HERMOGENES: Desire is far stronger, Socrates.

SOCRATES: Don't you think then that many people would escape from Hades, if he didn't bind those who come to him with the strongest of shackles?

HERMOGENES: Clearly.

SOCRATES: So, if he is to bind them with the strongest of shackles, rather than holding them by force, he must, it seems, bind them with some sort of desire.   —⟶ Hades

HERMOGENES: Evidently.

SOCRATES: Now, there are lots of desires, aren't there?

---

57. Because gold and silver are obtained from mines.

HERMOGENES: Yes.

SOCRATES: So, if he is really going to hold them with the greatest
d   shackles, he has to bind them with the greatest desire.

HERMOGENES: Yes.

SOCRATES: Is any desire greater than the desire to associate with
someone whose company one believes will make one a better
man?

HERMOGENES: No, there certainly isn't, Socrates.

SOCRATES: So let's say that it is for these reasons, Hermogenes,
that hitherto no one has wished to come back here from there.
e   The words Hades knows how to speak are so beautiful, it seems,
that everyone—even the Sirens—has been overcome by his en-
chantments. On this account, therefore, this god is a perfect
sophist, and a great benefactor to those who are with him.[58] So
great is the wealth that surrounds him there below, indeed, that
he even sends many good things to us from it. This is how he
got the name Pluto.[59] On the other hand, because he is unwill-
ing to associate with human beings while they have their bodies, but converses with them only when their souls are purified
404a   of all the desires and evils of the body, doesn't he seem to you to
be a philosopher? For hasn't he well understood that when people are free of their bodies he can bind them with the desire for
virtue, but that while they feel the agitation and madness of the
body not even the famous shackles of his father Kronos could
keep them with him?[60]

---

58. Like the sophists, Hades enchants or bewitches (*katakekêlêsthai*) his
associates by the power of his words (cf. *Protagoras* 315b), because of
their desire (313d, 318a) to become better people through associating
with him (316c, 318a).
59. See 403a.
60. Kronos, the father of Poseidon and Zeus, was dethroned by the latter and chained by him in Tartarus, the deepest part of Hades. See *Iliad*
14.203–4.

HERMOGENES: Probably so, Socrates.

SOCRATES: It's much more likely then, Hermogenes, that Hades   *b*
derives his name not from what cannot be seen (*aeides*), but from
the fact that he knows (*eidenai*) everything fine and beautiful,
and that that is why the rule-setter called him 'Hades'.

HERMOGENES: All right. But what about Demeter, Hera, Apollo,
Athena, Hephaestus, and all the other gods? What are we to say
about them?

SOCRATES: Demeter seems to have been so called because she
gives (*didousa*) nourishment just like a mother (*mêtêr*); Hera is a
lovable one (*eratê*), and, indeed, Zeus is said to have married her
for love. But perhaps the rule-setter, being a lofty thinker,[61]   *c*
called her 'Hera' as a disguised name for air (*aêr*), putting the
end of her name at the beginning—you'll get the idea if you re-
peat the name 'Hera' over and over. As for *'pherrephatta'*: it
seems that many people dread the names 'Pherrephatta' and
'Apollo' because they are ignorant about the correctness of
names, for they change the first name to 'Phersephone', and
then it seems terrifying to them.[62] But really the name 'Pherrephatta' indicates that the goddess is wise—for since things are
being swept along,[63] wisdom is the power to grasp (*epha-*   *d*
ptomenon), comprehend (*epaphaôn*), and follow (*epakolouthein*)
them. Thus it would be correct to call this goddess 'Pherepa-
pha', or something like that, because of her wisdom, that is to
say, her power to comprehend what is being swept along (*epaphê*
tou phereomenou)—this is also the reason that Hades, since he is
himself wise, associates with her. But people nowadays attach
more importance to euphony than to truth, so they distort her
name and call her 'Pherrephatta'. And, as I said, the same thing
has happened to Apollo. Many people are afraid of his name be-   *e*

---

61. *Meteôrologôn*: See 401b.
62. Presumably because they see it as meaning "who brings carnage"
(*pherein phonon*).
63. See *Republic* 402c.

cause they think it indicates something terrifying.[64] Haven't you noticed this?

HERMOGENES: I certainly have, and what you say is true.

SOCRATES: In my view, however, the name is most beautifully suited to the power of the god.

HERMOGENES: How so?

405a SOCRATES: I'll try to say how it seems to me, at least. I think no single name could be more in keeping with the four powers of the god. It comprehends each of them, expressing his power in music, prophecy, medicine, and archery. Apollos name is perfectly fitting

HERMOGENES: It's a pretty remarkable name you're talking about; so go ahead and explain it.

SOCRATES: It's certainly a harmonious one. After all, it's the name of the god of music. To begin with, the purgations and purifications that doctors and prophets use, the fumigations
b with medicinal and magical drugs, and the various washings and sprinklings that are involved in these processes, all have the same effect, don't they, namely, to make a person pure in body and soul?

HERMOGENES: Certainly.

SOCRATES: But isn't Apollo the purifying god who washes away (*apolouôn*) such evil impurities and releases (*apoluôn*) us from them?

HERMOGENES: Certainly.

SOCRATES: Since he washes and releases and is a doctor for our evil impurities, he might correctly be called *'Apolouôn'* ('The
c Washer'). On the other hand, it may well be most correct to call

---

64. They connect 'Apollo' with *'apolluôn'* ('the one who destroys').

him by the name the Thessalians use, since it accords with his prophecy, that is to say, with his single-mindedness (*haploun*) or truthfulness (these being the same thing), for all the Thessalians call this god *'Aploun'*. And since he always (*aei*) makes his shots (*bolôn*), because of his skill in archery, he is also *'Aeiballôn'* ('Always-shooting'). To understand how his name accords with his musical powers, we have to understand that the letter *'a'* often signifies togetherness (*to homou*), as it does in *'akolouthos'* ('follower' or 'attendant') and *'akoitis'* ('bed-fellow', 'spouse', 'husband').[65] In this case, it signifies moving together (*homou polêsis*), whether the moving together of the heavens around what we call the 'poles' (*'poloi'*), or the harmonious moving together in music, which we call 'being in concert' (*'sumphonia'*); for, as those who are clever in astronomy and music say, all these things move together simultaneously by a kind of harmony. Apollo is the god who directs the harmony, and makes all things move together (*homopolôn*), whether for gods or human beings. So, just as the names *'akolouthos'* and *'akoitis'* are derived from *'homokolouthos'* and *'homokoitis'* by replacing *'homo'* with *'a'*, we called him 'Apollo', though he was really *'Homopolôn'* ('the one who makes things move together'). We inserted the second *'l'* *e* lest his name become an oppressive one.[66] Even as it is, indeed, some people, who haven't correctly investigated the force or power of his name, are afraid of it, because they suspect that it does signify some kind of destructiveness. But, as we said earlier, it really comprehends each of the powers of the god, who is *406a* a single-minded, always-shooting washer, who makes things move together. As for the Muses and music and poetry in general, they seem to have derived their name from their eager desire (*môsthai*) to investigate and do philosophy. Leto is so-called because of being very gentle (*pra(i)otêtos*) and willing (*ethelêmos*) to do whatever is asked of her. Or perhaps her name derives from the one used by those who speak dialects other than Attic, many of whom call her 'Letho'—apparently on account of the fact that her character isn't rough but gentle and smooth (*leion*).

d

---

65. Reading *hôsper ton 'akolouthon' te kai tên 'akoitin'* with Duke et al.
66. *'Apolôn'* means 'destroying utterly', 'killing', 'slaying'.

b   Artemis appears to have been so-called because of her sound-
ness (*artemes*) and orderliness, and because of her desire for vir-
ginity (*parthenia*). Or perhaps the one who gave her that name
was calling her 'an investigator of virtue' (*'aretês histôr'*) or 'a
hater of sexual intercourse between men and women' (*'aroton
misêsasês'*). It is for some one of these reasons or for all of them
that the one who gave this name to the goddess gave it to her.

HERMOGENES: What about 'Dionysos' and 'Aphrodite'?

SOCRATES: You're asking great things of me, son of Hipponicus,
because there is not only a serious way of explaining the names
of these divinities but a playful one as well. You'll have to ask
c   others for the serious one, but there's nothing to prevent us from
going through the playful one—even the gods love play.
Dionysos, the giver of wine (*ho didous ton oinon*), might playfully
be called *'Didoinusos'*; while wine (*oinos*) would most justly be
called *'oionous'*, since it makes most drinkers think they understand (*oiesthai noun echein*) when they don't. As far as Aphrodite
is concerned, there's no point in contradicting Hesiod—we
should agree with him that she is called 'Aphrodite' because she
d   was born from foam (*aphros*).[67]

HERMOGENES: Being an Athenian, Socrates, you surely aren't
going to forget Athena, or Hephaestus and Ares either, for that
matter.

SOCRATES: Not likely.

HERMOGENES: No, indeed.

SOCRATES: It isn't hard to explain how Athena got her other
name.

HERMOGENES: Which one?

SOCRATES: 'Pallas'—you know we call her that.

---

67. *Theogony,* 195–7.

HERMOGENES: Of course.

SOCRATES: In my view, we would be correct to think that this name derives from her dancing in arms and armor, for lifting oneself or anything else up, whether from the ground or in one's hands, is called 'shaking' (*'pallein'*) and 'dancing' or 'being shaken' (*'pallesthai'*) and 'being danced'.   *e*

    407a

HERMOGENES: Certainly.

SOCRATES: She's called 'Pallas' because of this.

HERMOGENES: And correctly so. But how do you explain her other name?

SOCRATES: You mean 'Athena'?

HERMOGENES: Yes.

SOCRATES: That's a much weightier issue, my friend. The ancients seem to have had the same opinion about Athena as do contemporary experts on Homer. Many of them say in their interpretations of the poet that he represents Athena as Understanding or Thought. The maker of names seems to think the same sort of thing about the goddess. Indeed, he speaks of her in still grander terms, saying she is the very mind of god (*theou noêsis*), as if she is '*ha theonoa*'—using '*a*' in the non-Attic style in place of '*ê*' and deleting '*i*' and '*s*'.[68] But perhaps this isn't the explanation. Perhaps what he called her was '*Theonoê*', because of her unparalleled knowledge of divine things (*ta theia noousa*). Nor would we be far off the mark if we supposed that what he called her was '*Êthonoê*', because he wanted to identify the goddess with her understanding character (*hê en tô êthei noêsis*).   *b*

---

68. I.e., '*ha theonoa*' or 'Athena' is derived thus: delete '*sis*' from '*theou noêsis*', yielding a single word '*theounoê*'; add the feminine article in its non-Attic style and change '*ê*' to '*a*' to get '*ha theounoa*'. Since at this time there was not the distinction we now make between '*o*' and '*ou*', we get '*ha theonoa*'.

c Then he himself or others after him made the name more beautiful, as they thought, and called her *'Athênaa'*.

HERMOGENES: What about Hephaestus? How do you explain him?

SOCRATES: Are you asking me about the noble judge of light
(*phaeos histôr*)?

HERMOGENES: It seems so.

SOCRATES: Isn't it clear to everyone then that he is 'Phaestus',
with an *'ê'* added on?

HERMOGENES: It probably is—unless you happen to have yet another opinion on the matter. And you probably do.

SOCRATES: Then to prevent me from giving it, ask me about Ares.

HERMOGENES: Consider yourself asked!

SOCRATES: All right, if that's what you want. It is proper for a
god who is in every way warlike to be called 'Ares', for 'Ares'
d accords with virility (*arren*) and courage (*andreia*), or with a hard
and unbending nature, the one that is called *'arratos'*.

HERMOGENES: It certainly is.

SOCRATES: Then for god's sake let's leave the subject of the gods,
because it frightens me to talk about them. But ask me about
anything else you like, "until we see what the horses" of Euthyphro "can do."[69]

---

69. *Iliad* 5.221–2. For Euthyphro, see 396d. The association of Euthyphro's wisdom with horses is the beginning of an extended simile in
which the pursuit of truth is likened to a chariot race, e.g., "going beyond the trenches" (413a), "go off course" (414b), "coming to the finishing post" (420d). The simile is also used by Parmenides, and Plato may
well be alluding to him.

HERMOGENES: I'll do that, but there is still one god I want to ask you about, and that's Hermes, since Cratylus says that I am no   *e* Hermogenes (Son-of-Hermes).[70] So let's examine the name 'Hermes' and its meaning, to see whether there's anything in what he says.

SOCRATES: Well, the name 'Hermes' seems to have something to do with speech: he is an interpreter (*hermêneus*), a messenger, a thief and a deceiver in words, a wheeler-dealer—and all these   *408a* activities involve the power of speech. Now, as we mentioned before,[71] *'eirein'* means 'to use words', and the other part of the name says—as Homer often does—*'emêsato'* ('he contrived'), which means 'to devise'. And it was out of these two words that the rule-setter established the name of the god who devised speech (*legein*) and words, since *'eirein'* means the same as *'legein'* ('to speak'). It's just as if he had told us: "Humans, it would be right for you to call the god who has contrived speech (*to eirein emêsato*) *'Eiremês'*." But we, beautifying the name, as we   *b* suppose, call him 'Hermes' nowadays.

HERMOGENES: I'm certain that Cratylus was right when he said that I'm no Hermogenes then, since I'm no good at devising speeches.

SOCRATES: But it *is* reasonable for Pan to be Hermes' double-natured son.

HERMOGENES: How so?   *c*

SOCRATES: You know speech signifies all things (*to pan*) and keeps them circulating and always going about, and that it has two forms—true and false?

HERMOGENES: Certainly.

---

70. See n. 4 above.
71. See 398e.

SOCRATES: Well, the true part is smooth and divine and dwells among the gods above, while the false part dwells below among the human masses, and is rough and goatish (*tragikon*); for it is here, in the tragic (*tragikon*) life, that one finds the vast majority of myths and falsehoods.[72]

HERMOGENES: Certainly.

SOCRATES: Therefore the one who expresses all things (*pan*) and keeps them always in circulation (*aei polôn*) is correctly called 'Pan-the-goat-herd' ('*Pan aipolos*'). The double-natured son of Hermes, he is smooth in his upper parts, and rough and goatish in the ones below. He is either speech itself or the brother of speech, since he is the son of Hermes. And it's not a bit surprising that a brother resembles his brother. But, as I said, let's leave the gods.

d

HERMOGENES: That sort of gods, Socrates, if that's what you want. But what keeps you from discussing these gods: the sun and moon, and stars, earth, aither, air, fire, water, and the seasons and the year?[73]

e

SOCRATES: That's a lot you're asking of me! All the same, if it will please you, I am willing.

HERMOGENES: Of course, it will.

SOCRATES: Which one do you want me to take up first? Or, since you mentioned the sun (*hêlios*) first, shall we begin with it?

HERMOGENES: Certainly.

SOCRATES: If we use the Doric form of the name, I think matters will become clearer, for the Dorians call the sun '*halios*'. So '*halios*' might accord with the fact that the sun collects (*halizein*) people

409a

---

72. '*Tragôdia*' originally meant the song sung at the sacrifice of a goat. The adjective '*tragikon*' means either 'goat-like' or 'tragic'.
73. See *Phaedo* 109b, *Timaeus* 58d.

together when it rises, or with the fact that it is always rolling (*aei heilein iôn*) in its course around the earth, or with the fact that it seems to color (*poikillei*) the products of the earth, for '*poikillein*' means the same as '*aiolein*' ('to shift rapidly to and fro').[74]

HERMOGENES: What about the moon (*selênê*)?

SOCRATES: The name certainly seems to put Anaxagoras in an awkward position.

HERMOGENES: Why is that?

SOCRATES: It seems to reveal that his recent theory about the moon deriving its light from the sun is in fact quite old.

b

HERMOGENES: In what way?

SOCRATES: *Selas* (bright light) and *phôs* (light) are the same thing.

HERMOGENES: Yes.

SOCRATES: Now, if what the Anaxagoreans say is true, the light (*phôs*, i.e. *selas*) of the moon (*selênê*) is always both new (*neon*) and old (*henon*), for they say that as the sun circles around the moon it always casts new light on it, but that the light from the previous month also remains there.

HERMOGENES: Certainly.

SOCRATES: But many people call the moon '*Selanaia*'.

HERMOGENES: Yes, they do.

SOCRATES: And, since its light is always both new and old (*selas*

---

74. In the active '*aiolein*' means 'to shift rapidly to and fro', and is therefore somewhat close in meaning to '*heilein*'; in the passive it means 'to change in color or hue' and so is close in meaning to '*poikillein*'.

neon kai enon echei aei), it would be right to call it '*Sela-*
c   *enoneoaeia*',[75] which has been compressed into '*Selanaia*'.

HERMOGENES: And a dithyrambic[76] name it is too, Socrates! But
what have you to say about the month and the stars?

SOCRATES: The correct name to call a month (*meis*) is '*meiês*' from
'*meiousthai*' ('to grow smaller'). And the stars (*astra*) seem to get
their name given to them from '*astrapê*' ('lightning'), for lightning is what causes the eyes to turn upward (*anastrephei ta ôpa*).
Hence, it should really be called '*anastrôpê*', but nowadays the
name is beautified and it is called '*astrapê*'.[77]

HERMOGENES: What about fire and water?

SOCRATES: I'm really puzzled about fire (*pur*). So either Euthy-
d   phro's muse has abandoned me or this really is very hard. But
notice the device I use in all such puzzling cases.

HERMOGENES: What is that?

SOCRATES: I'll tell you. But first answer me this. Could you say
in what way *pur* (fire) comes to be so called?

HERMOGENES: I certainly can't.

SOCRATES: Here's what I suspect. I think that the Greeks, espe-
e   cially those who live abroad, have adopted many names from
foreign tongues.

HERMOGENES: What of it?

SOCRATES: Well, if someone were trying to discover whether
these names had been reasonably given, and he treated them as

---

75. Omitting *tôn onomatôn* with Duke et al.
76. A dithyramb is a choral song to the god Dionysus, noted for its
complex and pompous language.
77. See 404d.

belonging to the Greek language rather than the one they really come from, you know that he would be in a quandary.

HERMOGENES: He very probably would.

SOCRATES: Now, look at 'fire' (*'pur'*) and see whether it isn't a *410a* foreign name—for it certainly isn't easy to connect it with the Greek language. Besides, it's obvious that the Phrygians use the same name slightly altered. And the same holds for 'water' (*'hudôr'*) and 'dog' (*'kuôn'*), and lots of others.

HERMOGENES: So it does.

SOCRATES: Consequently, though one might say something about these names, one mustn't push them too far. That, then, is how I get rid of 'fire' (*'pur'*) and 'water' (*'hudôr'*). But what about air, Hermogenes? Is it called *'aêr'* because it raises (*airei*) things *b* from the earth? Or because it is always flowing (*aei rhei*)? Or because wind (*pneuma*) arises from its flow? For the poets call the winds (*pneumata*) 'gales' (*'aêtai'*), don't they? So, perhaps a poet says *'aêtorrous'* ('gale flow') in place of *'pneumatorrous'* ('wind flow'), thereby indicating that what he is talking about is air.[78] As for aither, I'd explain it as follows: it is right to call it *'aei-theêr'*, because it is always running and flowing (*aei thei rheôn*)

---

78. I have translated *hothen dê bouletai auton houtôs eipein, hoti estin aêr,* which Burnet brackets and Duke et al. omit. Plato seems to have the following in mind. The fact that the wind arises from X's flow gives us a reason to call X *'aêr'*, because the poets call the winds 'gales' (*'aêtas'*). But how? *'Pneumatorroun'* is a compound of *'pneuma'* (air) and *'rhein'* (to flow). In the same way, *'aêtorroun'*, a Platonic coinage, is to be taken as a compound of *'aêtai'* and *'rhein'*. On the hypothesis that a poet would use *'aêtorroun'* in place of *'pneumatorroun'*, if he uses *'aêtai'* in place of *'pneumata'*, we get that *'pneumatorroun'* and *'aêtorroun'* signify the same thing. But if *pneumata* are flowing air, then *'pneumata'* is an abbreviation of *'pneumatorroun'*. So it is plausible to think that *'aêr'* is an abbreviation of *'aêtorroun'*. But abbreviations of words that signify the same thing also signify the same thing. So if *pneumata* are flowing air, then *aêr* is flowing air! So if the wind arises from X's flow, it is reasonable to call X *'aêr'*.

about the air. The earth (*gê*) is better signified by the name *'gaia'*;
c   for *gaia* is correctly called a 'mother', as Homer tells us by using
'gegaasi' for 'to be born'. All right, what was to come next?

HERMOGENES: 'Seasons' (*'Hôrai'*), Socrates, and the two names
for the year, *'eniautos'* and *'etos'*.

SOCRATES: If you want to know the probable truth about the
name *'hôrai'* ('seasons'), you must look to the fact that it is
spelled *'horai'* in old Attic. The seasons are rightly called *'horai'*
('things that distinguish or mark off one thing from another'),
because they distinguish (*horizein*) the weathers of winter and
summer, the winds, and the fruits of the earth. As for *'eniautos'*
d   and *'etos'*, they are actually one name. We saw earlier that Zeus'
name was divided in two—some called him *'Zêna'*, some *'Dia'* in
the accusative.[79] Well, exactly the same is true of the name of the
year. It is the year by itself that brings the plants and animals of
the earth to light, each in its proper season, and passes them in
review within itself (*en heautô(i) exetazei*). Hence, some people
call it *'etos'*, because it passes things in review (*etazei*), while others call it *'eniautos'*, because it does this within itself (*en
heautô(i)*). The whole phrase is 'passing things in review within
itself' (*'en heautô(i) etazon'*), but this single phrase results in the
year being called these two different names. Thus, the two
e   names, *'eniautos'* and *'etos'*, derive from a single phrase.

HERMOGENES: I say, Socrates, you *are* making great progress!

SOCRATES: I think I'm driving my apparent wisdom pretty hard
at present.

HERMOGENES: You certainly are.

SOCRATES: You'll be even more certain in a second.

411a   HERMOGENES: Now that we've examined that sort of name, I'd
next like to see with what correctness the names of the virtues

---

79. See 395e ff.

are given. I mean 'wisdom' ('phronêsis'), 'comprehension' ('sunesis'), 'justice' ('dikaiosunê'), and all the other fine names of that sort.

SOCRATES: That's no inconsequential class of names you're stirring up, Hermogenes, but, since I have put on the lion's skin,[80] I mustn't lose heart. So, it seems I must investigate 'wisdom', 'comprehension', 'judgment' ('gnômê'), 'knowledge' ('epistêmê'), and all those other fine names of which you speak.   *b*

HERMOGENES: We certainly mustn't stop until we've done so.

SOCRATES: By the dog, I think that's a pretty good inspiration— what popped into my mind just now![81] Most of our wise men nowadays get so dizzy going around and around in their search for the nature of the things that are, that the things themselves appear to them to be turning around and moving every which way. Well, I think that the people who gave things their names in very ancient times are exactly like these wise men.[82] They   *c* don't blame this on their own internal condition, however, but on the nature of the things themselves, which they think are never stable or steadfast, but flowing and moving, full of every sort of motion and constant coming into being. I say this, because the names you just mentioned put me in mind of it.

HERMOGENES: How did they do that, Socrates?

SOCRATES: Perhaps you didn't notice that they are given on the assumption that the things they name are moving, flowing, and coming into being.

HERMOGENES: No, I didn't think of that at all.

SOCRATES: Well, to begin with, the first name we mentioned is   *d* undoubtedly like this.

---

80. The skin of the Nemean lion worn by Heracles.
81. See 396d ff.
82. See 401d ff.

HERMOGENES: What name was that?

SOCRATES: 'Wisdom' (*'phronêsis'*). Wisdom is the understanding of motion (*phoras noêsis*) and flow. Or it might be interpreted as taking delight in motion (*phoras onêsis*). In either case, it has to do with motion. If you want another example, the name 'judgment' (*'gnômê'*) expresses the fact that to judge is to examine or study whatever is begotten (*gonês nômêsis*); for 'studying' (*'nôman'*) and 'examining' (*'skopein'*) are the same. And if you want yet another example, understanding (*noêsis*) itself is the longing for the new (*neou hesis*). But to say that the things that are are new is to signify that they are always coming into being. And such things are what the soul longs for, as the giver of the name, *'neoesis'* expressed, for the ancient name wasn't *'noêsis'* but *'noeesis'*, but an *'ê'* took the place of the double *'e'*.[83] Moderation (*sôphrosunê*) is the savior (*sôteria*) of the wisdom (*phronêsis*) we just looked at. 'Knowledge' (*'epistêmê'*) indicates that a worthwhile soul follows (*hepetai*) the movement of things, neither falling behind nor running on ahead. So we ought to insert an *'h'* in the name and spell it *'hepistêmê'*.[84] Comprehension (*sunesis*), in turn, seems to be a kind of summing up (*sullogismos*), and whenever one says 'comprehends' (*'sunienai'*), it's exactly as if one has said 'knows' (*'epistasthai'*), for *'sunienai'* (literally, 'goes along with') means that the soul 'journeys together' with things. As for 'wisdom' (*'sophia'*), it signifies the grasp of motion.[85] But it is rather obscure and non-Attic. Nonetheless, we must remember that the poets often say of something that begins to advance quickly that it "rushed" (*"esuthê"*). Indeed, there was a famous Spartan man named *'Sous'*, for this is what the Spartans call a rapid advance. 'Wisdom' signifies the grasping (*epaphê*) of this motion, on the assumption that the things that are are moving. The name 'good' (*'agathon'*) is intended to signify everything in nature that is admirable (*agaston*). The things that are are moving, but some are moving quickly, others slowly.

---

83. Apparently the original *'neoesis'* became *'noeesis'* by inversion of the letters *'eo'*, then *'noêsis'*.
84. Reading *hepistêmen* with Duke et al.
85. See 404d.

So what moves quickly is not all there is, but the admirable part of it. Hence this name *'tagathon'* ('the good') is applied to what is admirable (*agaston*) about the fast (*thoon*).[86]

It's easy to figure out that 'justice' (*'dikaiosunê'*) is the name given to the comprehension of the just (*dikaiou sunesis*), but the just itself is hard to understand. It seems that many people agree with one another about it up to a point, but beyond that they disagree. Those who think that the universe is in motion believe   *d* that most of it is of such a kind as to do nothing but give way, but that something penetrates all of it and generates everything that comes into being. This, they say, is the fastest and smallest thing of all; for if it were not the smallest, so that nothing could keep it out, or not the fastest, so that it could treat all other things as though they were standing still, it wouldn't be able to travel through everything. However, since it is governor and penetrator (*diaion*) of everything else, it is rightly called 'just' (*'dikaïon'*)—the *'k'*-sound is added for the sake of euphony. As I   *e* was saying before, many people agree about the just up to this point. As for myself, Hermogenes, because I persisted at it, I   *413a* learned all about the matter in secret[87]—that this is the just and the cause of everything that comes into being, since that through which (*di' ho*) a thing comes to be is the cause. Indeed, someone told me that it is correct to call this *'Dia'* ('Zeus') for that reason. Even when I'd heard this, however, I persisted in gently asking, "If all this is true, my friend, what actually *is* the just?" Thereupon, they think I am asking too many questions and demanding the impossible,[88] and they tell me that I have already learned   *b* enough. Then they try to satisfy me by having each tell me his own view. But they disagree with each other. One says that the just is the sun, since only the sun governs all of the things that are, penetrating (*diaïôn*) and burning (*kaôn*) them. Well-satisfied,

---

86. The mss. text is corrupt here, but this seems to be the best guess as to the meaning. I translate Burnet's text, which is also adopted by Duke et al.

87. See *Theaetetus* 152c ff.

88. Literally: "going beyond the trenches (*huper ta eskammena*)." Trenches marked the boundaries in chariot races.

I tell this fine answer to one of the others, but he ridicules me by asking if I think nothing just ever happens in human affairs once the sun has set. So I persist, and ask him to tell me what he

c   thinks the just is, and he says that it is fire (*to pur*)—but that isn't easy to understand. Another says that it isn't fire, but the heat itself that is in fire. Another says that all these explanations are ridiculous, and that the just is what Anaxagoras talks about, namely, mind; for he says that mind is self-ruling, mixes with nothing else, orders the things that are, and travels through everything. Thereupon, my friend, I am even more perplexed than when I set out to learn what the just is.[89] However, the goal

d   of our investigation was the *name* 'just', and it seems to have been given for the reasons we mentioned.

HERMOGENES: I think you really must have heard this from someone, Socrates, rather than making it up as you went along.

SOCRATES: What about the other explanations I've mentioned?

HERMOGENES: I certainly don't think you heard those.

SOCRATES: Listen, then, and perhaps I'll be able to deceive you into thinking that I haven't heard the remaining ones either. After justice what's left? I don't think we've discussed courage—but it's clear that injustice (*adikia*) is really nothing more than a hindering of that which penetrates (*diaïôn*). 'Courage' ('*andreia*') signifies that this virtue was given its name

e   in battle. And if indeed the things that are are flowing, then a battle cannot be anything but an opposing flow. If we remove the '*d*' from '*andreia*' to get '*anreia*' ('flowing back'), the name itself indicates this fact. Of course, it is clear that courage doesn't oppose every flow, but only the one that is contrary to justice; otherwise, courage wouldn't be praiseworthy. Similarly, 'male'

414a   ('*arren*') and 'man' ('*anêr*') indicate upward flow (*anô rhoê*). It seems to me that '*gunê*' ('woman') wants to be '*gonê*' ('womb'), that '*thêlus*' ('female') comes from '*thêlê*' ('nipple'), and that a nipple (*thêlê*) is so-called, Hermogenes, because it makes things

---

89. Cf. *Phaedo* 96a–99d.

flourish (*tethêlenai*) in just the way that watering makes plants flourish.

HERMOGENES: Probably so, Socrates.

SOCRATES: Yes, '*thallein*' itself seems to me to be like the sudden and rapid growth of the young, for the name-giver has imitated something like this in the name, which he put together from   *b* '*thein*' ('to run') and '*hallesthai*' ('to jump'). Notice how I go off course, when I get on the flat.[90] But there are plenty of names left[91] that seem important.

HERMOGENES: That's true.

SOCRATES: And one of them is to see what the name '*technê*' ('craft') means.

HERMOGENES: Certainly.

SOCRATES: If you remove the '*t*' and insert an '*o*' between the '*ch*' and the '*n*' and the '*n*' and the '*ê*',[92] doesn't it signify the possession of understanding (*hexis nou*)?   *c*

HERMOGENES: Yes, Socrates, but getting it to do so is like trying to haul a boat up a very sticky ramp!

SOCRATES: But then you know, Hermogenes, that the first names given to things have long since been covered over by those who wanted to dress them up, and that letters were added or subtracted to make them sound good in the mouth, resulting in distortions and ornamentations of every kind. You know, too, that time has had a share in this process. Take '*katoptron*' ('mirror'), for example, don't you think that the '*r*' is an absurd addition?[93]

---

90. Socrates has gone off course, because 'male', 'female' etc. are not names of virtues.
91. Reading *loipa* with Duke et al.
92. Resulting in '*echonoê*'.
93. Because it interrupts the sequence '*opto*', suggesting a verb for seeing.

In my view, this sort of thing is the work of people who think
d nothing of the truth, but only of the sounds their mouths make.
Hence, they keep embellishing the first names, until finally a
name is reached that no human being can understand. One example, among many others, is that they call the Sphinx by that
name instead of '*Phix*'.[94]

HERMOGENES: That's right, Socrates.

SOCRATES: And yet, if we can add whatever we like to names, or
subtract whatever we like from them, it will be far too easy to fit
e any name to any thing.

HERMOGENES: That's true.

SOCRATES: Yes, it is true. So, I think a wise supervisor,[95] like
yourself, will have to keep a close watch, to preserve balance
and probability.

HERMOGENES: That's what I want to do.

SOCRATES: And I want to do it along with you, Hermogenes, but
415a don't demand too much precision, in case

> *You enfeeble my strength.*[96]

Now that '*technê*' is out of the way, I'm about to come to the
summit of our inquiries. But first I'll investigate '*mêchanê*' ('device'). It seems to me that '*mêchanê*' signifies great accomplish-
ment (*anein epi polu*); for '*mêkos*' signifies some sort of greatness,
and these two, '*mêkos*' and '*anein*' make up the name '*mêchanê*'.
But, as I was saying just now, we must go on to the summit of

---

94. Hesiod uses the latter form of the name at *Theogony* 326. Popular etymology inappropriately connects '*Sphigx*' with '*sphiggein*' ('to tor-
ture'). '*Phix*' connects it more appropriately with Mount Phikion in
Boeotia.
95. See 390b ff.
96. *Iliad* 6.265.

our inquiries, and investigate the names *'aretê'* ('virtue') and
'kakia' ('vice'). I don't yet understand the first of them, but the   *b*
other seems clear enough, since it is in harmony with everything
we said before. To the degree that things are in motion, all that is
moving badly (*kakôs ion*) should be called *'kakia'*, but the name for
all such things is mostly given to a soul in which this bad movement in relation to things resides. It seems to me that the name
'deilia' ('cowardice'), which we haven't discussed, expresses what
this bad movement is.—We ought to have discussed *'deilia'* after
'andreia' ('courage'), but we passed it by, as I believe we have   *c*
passed by lots of other names.—Now, *'deilia'* signifies the soul's
being bound with a strong shackle (*desmos*), for *lian* (too much) is
a degree of strength. Therefore, *'deilia'* signifies the strongest of
the soul's shackles. *Aporia* (perplexity, inability to move on)[97] is a
vice of the same sort, and so, it seems, is everything else that hinders movement and motion. This makes it clear that the bad
movement in question is a restrained or hindered motion, whose
possession by a soul causes it to become filled with vice. And, if
'kakia' is the name of that sort of thing, *'aretê'* is the opposite. It
signifies, first, lack of perplexity (*euporia*, ease of movement), and,   *d*
second, that the flow of a good soul is always unimpeded; for it
seems that it is given this name *'aretê'* because it is unrestrained
and unhindered and so is always flowing (*aei rheon*). Thus it is
correct to call it *'aeirheitê'*, but this has been contracted, and it is
called *'aretê'*. Now, maybe you'll say that I'm inventing things
again,[98] but I think that if what I just said about *'kakia'* is correct,
then so is what I said about the name *'aretê'*.   *e*

HERMOGENES: What about *'kakon'* ('bad'), which has been involved in many of the previous inquiries? What's the meaning   *416a*
of it?

SOCRATES: It's a strange word, by god! At least, that's what I
think. And one that's hard to interpret. So I'll use the device I introduced earlier on it as well.[99]

---

97. From *'poreuesthai'* ('to move').
98. See 413d.
99. See 409d.

HERMOGENES: Which one?

SOCRATES: That of attributing a foreign origin to it.

HERMOGENES: And you may well be correct. So suppose we leave these inquiries, and try to see what rationale there is for *'kalon'* ('fine', 'beautiful') and *'aischron'* ('disgraceful', 'ugly').

SOCRATES: The meaning of *'aischron'* seems clear to me, and it is
b   also in harmony with what we said before. It seems to me that the giver of names reviles everything that hinders or restrains the flowing of the things that are. In particular, he gave this name *'aeiscoroun'* to what always restrains their flowing (*aei ischei ton rhoun*). But nowadays it is contracted and pronounced *'aischron'*.

HERMOGENES: What about *'kalon'*?

SOCRATES: It's harder to understand.[100] Indeed, it is pronounced like this only because it sounds harmonious to shorten the *'ou'* to *'o'*.

HERMOGENES: How so?

SOCRATES: In my view, this name derives from a sort of thought (*dianoia*).

HERMOGENES: What do you mean?

c   SOCRATES: Tell me. What caused each of the things that are to be called by a name? Isn't it whatever gave them their names?

HERMOGENES: Certainly.

SOCRATES: And wasn't it thought—whether divine or human or both—that did this?

---

100. See 384b: "fine things are hard."

HERMOGENES: Yes.

SOCRATES: And isn't what originally named them the same as what names (*kaloun*) them now, that is to say, thought?

HERMOGENES: Evidently.

SOCRATES: Aren't all the works performed by thought and understanding praiseworthy, while those that aren't are blameworthy?

HERMOGENES: Certainly.

SOCRATES: Now, medicine performs medical works and carpentry performs works of carpentry? Do you agree?   *d*

HERMOGENES: I do.

SOCRATES: And to name things (*kaloun*) is to perform beautiful (*kalon*) works?

HERMOGENES: Necessarily.

SOCRATES: And we say that it is thought that does this?

HERMOGENES: Certainly.

SOCRATES: Therefore wisdom (*phronêsis*) is correctly given the name '*kalon*' ('beautiful'), since it performs the works that we say are beautiful and welcome as such.

HERMOGENES: Evidently.

SOCRATES: What other such names still remain for us to examine?   *e*

HERMOGENES: Those related to the good and the beautiful, such as '*sumpheron*' ('advantageous'), '*lusiteloun*' ('profitable'), '*ôphelimon*' ('beneficial'), '*kerdaleon*' ('gainful'), and their opposites.   *417a*

SOCRATES: In light of the previous investigations, you should

now be able to explain *'sumpheron'* ('advantageous') for yourself, since it is obviously a close relative of *'epistêmê'* ('knowledge'). It expresses the fact that what is advantageous is nothing
other than the movement (*phora*) of a soul in accord with the
movement of things.[101] The things that are done as a result of
this movement are probably called *'sumphora'* or *'sumpheronta'*
because they are being moved in harmony with things (*sumpe-
ripheresthai*). But *'kerdaleon'* ('gainful') derives from *'kerdos'*

b   ('gain'). If you replace the *'d'* in *'kerdos'* with an *'n'*, the name expresses its meaning clearly; it names the good, but in another
way. Because the good penetrates everything, it has the power
to regulate (*kerannutai*) everything,[102] and the one who gave it its
name named it after this power. But he put a *'d'* instead of the *'n'*
and pronounced it *'kerdos'*.

HERMOGENES: What about *'lusiteloun'* ('profitable')?

SOCRATES: I don't think, Hermogenes, that he uses the name
'lusiteloun' to mean the profit that releases (*apoluei*) a capital sum
for reinvestment, which is what retailers use it to mean. The
name-giver calls the good by that name because it is the fastest

c   of the things that are, it doesn't allow things to remain at rest, or
permit their motion to stop, pause, or reach an end. Instead, it
always does away with (*luei*) any attempt to let motion end,
making it unceasing and immortal. In my view, it is for this reason that the good is said to be *'lusiteloun'*, because it does away
with (*luon*) any end (*telos*) to motion. *'Ôphelimon'* ('beneficial') is
a non-Attic name. Homer often uses it in the form *'ophellein'*,
which derives from *'poiein auxên'*[103] ('to make grow').

d   HERMOGENES: And what are we to say about their opposites?

SOCRATES: Those that are mere negations don't need any discussion, in my view.

---

101. See 412a ff.
102. See 412b ff.
103. Reading *auxên poiein* with Duke et al.

HERMOGENES: Which ones are they?

SOCRATES: *'Asumpheron'* ('disadvantageous'), *'anôpheles'* ('non-beneficial'), *'alusiteles'* ('unprofitable'), and *'akerdes'* ('non-gainful').

HERMOGENES: It's true, they don't need discussion.

SOCRATES: But *'blaberon'* ('harmful') and *'zêmiôdes'* ('hurtful') do.

HERMOGENES: Yes.

SOCRATES: *'Blaberon'* ('harmful') means that which is harming (*blapton*) the flow (*rhoun*). *'Blapton'*, in turn, signifies wanting to   *e* grasp (*boulomenon haptein*).[104] But grasping is the same as shackling, and the name-giver always finds fault with that.[105] Now what wants to grasp the flow (*to boulomenon haptein rhoun*) would be most correctly called *'boulapteroun'*, but this has been beautified, as it seems to me, and so it is called *'blaberon'*.[106]

HERMOGENES: What intricate names you come up with, Socrates! When you uttered the name *'boulapteroun'* just now, you looked just as if you were whistling the flute-prelude of the Hymn to Athena!   *418a*

SOCRATES: I'm not responsible for them, Hermogenes; the name-givers are.

HERMOGENES: That's true. But what about *'zêmiôdes'* ('hurtful')? What does it mean?

SOCRATES: What does *'zêmiôdes'* mean? See how right I was to say, Hermogenes, that people make huge changes in the meaning of names by adding or subtracting letters, and how even a very slight alteration of this sort can make a name signify the

---

104. See 404d, 412b on wisdom.
105. See 415c, 402e, 403c ff.
106. See 404d, 409c.

opposite of what it used to signify. *'Deon'* ('obligation') is an ex-
b   ample that has just occurred to me, and it reminds me of what I
was about to say to you about *'zêmiôdes'*. This[107] fine modern
language of ours has obliterated the true meaning of these
names by so twisting them around that they now mean the opposite of what they used to, whereas the ancient language expresses clearly what they mean.

HERMOGENES: What do you mean?

SOCRATES: I'll tell you. You know that our ancestors made great
use of *'i'* and *'d'* (especially the women, who are the best pre-
c   servers of the ancient language). But nowadays people change
'i' to *'ê'* or *'e'*, which are supposed to sound more grandiose.

HERMOGENES: They do?

SOCRATES: Yes. For example, people now call the day *'hêmera'*,
but in very ancient times they called it *'himera'* or *'hemera'*.

HERMOGENES: That's true.

SOCRATES: You know then that only the ancient name expresses
the name-giver's meaning clearly? People welcome the daylight
d   that comes out of the darkness and long for (*himeirousin*) it, and
that's why they named it *'himera'*.

HERMOGENES: Evidently.

SOCRATES: But nowadays the name is so dressed up[108] that no
one can understand what it means. Although there are some
who think the day is called *'hêmera'* because it makes things gentle (*hêmera*).

HERMOGENES: So it seems.

---

107. Reading *hautê* with Duke et al.
108. See 414c.

SOCRATES: Do you also know that the ancients called a yoke *'duogon'* not *'zugon'*?

HERMOGENES: Of course.

SOCRATES: Now, *'zugon'* expresses nothing clearly, but the name *'duogon'*, on the other hand, is quite rightly given to whatever binds two animals together so that they can pull a plough or cart (*duoin agôgên*). Nonetheless, nowadays *'zugon'* it is. And there   *e* are plenty of other examples.

HERMOGENES: Evidently.

SOCRATES: Similarly, *'deon'* ('obligation'), when pronounced in this way, seems at first to signify the opposite of all the other names for the good. After all, even though an obligation is a kind of good, *'deon'* plainly signifies a shackle (*desmos*) and obstacle to motion, and so is closely akin to *'blaberon'* ('harmful').[109]

HERMOGENES: Yes, Socrates, it does plainly signify that.

SOCRATES: But not if you use the ancient name, which is much more likely to have been correctly given than the present one. If you replace the *'e'* with an *'i'*, as in the ancient name, it agrees   *419a* with the earlier names of good things[110]—for *'dion'* ('passing through'), not *'deon'*, signifies a good, and is a term of praise. So the name-giver didn't contradict himself, and *'deon'* ('obligation') is plainly the same as *'ôphelimon'* ('beneficial'), *'lusiteloun'* ('profitable'), *'kerdaleon'* ('gainful'), *'agathon'* ('good'), *'sumpheron'* ('advantageous'), and *'euporon'* ('lack of perplexity'),[111] which are different names signifying what orders and moves. This is always praised, while what restrains and shackles is found fault with. Likewise, in the case of *'zêmiôdes'* ('hurtful'), if you replace   *b* the *'z'* with a *'d'*, as in the ancient language, it will be plain to

---

109. See 417d.
110. See 418b ff.
111. See 415c–d.

you that the name was given to what shackles motion (*doun to ion*), since '*dêmiôdes*' derives from that.

HERMOGENES: What about '*hêdonê*' ('pleasure'), '*lupê*' ('pain'), and '*epithumia*' ('appetite'), Socrates, and others like them?

SOCRATES: I don't think there is any great difficulty about them, Hermogenes. '*Hêdonê*' ('pleasure') seems to have been given its name because it is an activity that tends towards enjoyment (*hê onêsis*), but a '*d*' has been inserted and we call it '*hêdonê*' instead of '*hêonê*'. '*Lupê*' ('pain') seems to derive from the weakening (*di-*

c *alusis*) the body suffers when in pain. '*Ania*' ('sorrow') signifies what hinders (*hienai*) motion. '*Algêdôn*' ('distress') seems to me to be a foreign name deriving from '*algeinos*' ('distressing'). '*Odunê*' ('grief') seems to be named after the entering in (*endusis*) of pain. It is clear to everyone that pronouncing the name '*achthêdôn*' ('affliction') is like giving motion a burden (*achthos*) to carry.[112] '*Chara*' ('joy') seems to have been so called because it is an outpouring (*diachusis*) or good movement[113] of the soul's flow (*rhoê*). '*Terpsis*' ('delight') comes from '*terpnon*' ('delight-

d ful'), which, in turn, comes from that which glides (*herpsis*) through the soul like a breath (*pnoê*). By rights it is called '*herp-noun*', but over time its name has been changed to '*terpnon*'. '*Eu-phrosunê*' ('lightheartedness') needs no explanation, since it is clear to everyone that it derives its name from the movement of the soul that well accords (*eu sumphêresthai*) with that of things. By rights it is called '*eupherosunê*', but we call it '*euphrosunê*'. Nor is there any difficulty about '*epithumia*' ('appetite'), for it is clear that its name derives from the power that opposes the spirited part of the soul (*epi ton thumon iousa*),[114] while '*thumos*' ('spirit', 'anger') derives from the raging (*thusis*) and boiling of the

e soul.[115] The name '*himeros*' ('desire') derives from what most drives the soul's flow. It flows with a rush (*hiemenos rhei*) and sets on (*ephiemenos*) things, thus violently dragging the soul be-

---

112. See 414a.
113. *Euporia*: See 415c ff.
114. See *Republic* 439e–441c.
115. See *Timaeus* 70b ff.

cause of the rush of its flow. And so, because it has all this 420a
power, it is called '*himeros*'. '*Pothos*' ('longing'), on the other
hand, signifies that it isn't a desire (or flow) for what is present
but for what is elsewhere (*pou*) or absent. So, when its object is
absent, it is given the name '*pothos*', and, when its object is present, it is called '*himeros*'. '*Erôs*' ('erotic love') is so called because
it flows in from outside, that is to say, the flow doesn't belong to
the person who has it, but is introduced into him through his b
eyes. Because of this it was called '*esros*' ('influx') in ancient
times, when they used '*o*' for '*ô*', but now that '*o*' is changed to
'*ô*', it is called '*erôs*'. So, what other names do you think are left
for us to examine?

HERMOGENES: What do you think about '*doxa*' ('opinion') and
the like?

SOCRATES: '*Doxa*' ('opinion') either derives from the pursuit
(*diôxis*) the soul engages in when it hunts for the knowledge of
how things are, or it derives from the shooting of a bow (*toxon*).
But the latter is more likely. At any rate, '*oiêsis*' ('thinking') is in
harmony with it. It seems to express the fact that thinking is the c
motion (*oisis*) of the soul towards every thing, towards how each
of the things that are really is. In the same way, '*boulê*' ('planning') has to do with trying to hit (*bolê*) some target, and
'*boulesthai*' ('wishing') and '*bouleuesthai*' ('deliberating') signify
aiming at something (*ephiesthai*). All these names seem to go
along with '*doxa*' in that they're all like '*bolê*', like trying to hit
some target. Similarly, the opposite, '*aboulia*' ('lack of planning'),
seems to signify a failure to get something (*atuchia*), as when
someone fails to hit or get what he shot at, wished for, planned,
or desired.

HERMOGENES: The pace of investigating seems to be quickening,
Socrates! d

SOCRATES: That's because I'm coming to the finishing post! But I
still want to investigate '*anagkê*' ('compulsion') and '*hekousion*'
('voluntary'), since they're next. The name '*hekousion*' expresses
the fact that it signifies yielding and not resisting, but yielding,
as I said before, to the motion (*eikon tô(i) ionti*)—the one that

comes into being in accord with our wish. *'Anagkaion'* ('compulsory') and *'antitupnon'* ('resistant'), on the other hand, since they signify motion contrary to our wish, are associated with 'error' and 'ignorance'. Indeed, saying *'anagkaion'* is like trying to get through a ravine (*agkê*), for ravines restrain motion, since they
e are rough-going, filled with bushes, and hard to get through. It's probably for this reason that we use *'anagkaion'* in the way we do—because saying it is like trying to get through a ravine. Nonetheless, while my strength lasts, let's not stop using it. Don't you stop, either, but keep asking your questions.

HERMOGENES: Well, then, let me ask about the finest and most
421a important names, *'alêtheia'* ('truth'), *'pseudos'* ('falsehood'), *'on'* ('being'), and—the subject of our present conversation—*'onoma'* ('name'), and why it is so named.

SOCRATES: Do you know what *'maiesthai'* means?

HERMOGENES: Yes, it means 'to search' (*'zêtein'*).

SOCRATES: Well, *'onoma'* ('name') seems to be a compressed statement which says: "this is a being for which there is a search." You can see this more easily in *'onomaston'* ('thing named'), since it clearly says: "this is a being for which there is a search (*on hou masma estin*)." *'Alêtheia'* ('truth') is like these oth-
b ers in being compressed, for the divine motion of being is called *'alêtheia'* because *'alêtheia'* is a compressed form of the phrase "a wandering that is divine (*alê theia*)." *'Pseudos'* ('falsehood') is the opposite of this motion, so that, once again, what is restrained or compelled to be inactive is reviled by the name-giver, and likened to people asleep (*katheudousi*)—but the meaning of the name is concealed by the addition of *'ps'*. *'On'* ('being') or *'ousia'* ('being') says the same as *'alêtheia'* once an *'i'* is added, since it signifies going (*ion*). *'Ouk on'* ('not being'), in turn, is *'ouk ion'* ('not
c going'), and indeed some people actually use that name for it.

HERMOGENES: I think you've hammered these into shape manfully, Socrates. But suppose someone were to ask you about the correctness of the names *'ion'* ('going'), *'rheon'* ('flowing'), and *'doun'* ('shackling') . . .

SOCRATES: "How should we answer him?" Is that what you were going to say?

HERMOGENES: Yes, exactly.

SOCRATES: One way of giving the semblance of an answer has been suggested already.[116]

HERMOGENES: What way is that?

SOCRATES: To say that a name has a foreign origin when we don't know what it signifies. Now, it may well be true that some of these names are foreign, but it is also possible that the basic or *d* 'first' names are Greek, but not recoverable because they are so old. Names have been twisted in so many ways, indeed, that it wouldn't be surprising if the ancient Greek word was the same as the modern foreign one.

HERMOGENES: At any rate, it wouldn't be at all inappropriate for you to respond that way.

SOCRATES: No, because what I am saying is plausible. Nevertheless, it seems to me that "once we're in the competition, we're allowed no excuses,"[117] but must investigate these names vigorously. We should remember this, however: if someone asks about the terms from which a name is formed, and then about *e* the ones from which those terms are formed, and keeps on doing this indefinitely, the answerer must finally give up. Mustn't he?

HERMOGENES: That's my view, at any rate.   *422a*

SOCRATES: At what point would he be right to stop? Wouldn't it be when he reaches the names that are as it were the elements of all the other statements and names? For, if these are indeed elements, it cannot be right to suppose that *they* are composed out of other names. Consider *'agathos'* ('good'), for example; we said

---

116. See 409d ff., 416a ff.
117. A proverbial expression. See Plato, *Laws* 751d.

it is composed out of *'agaston'* ('admirable') and *'thoon'* ('fast').[118] And probably *'thoon'* is composed out of other names, and those out of still other ones. But if we ever get hold of a name that isn't *b* composed out of other names, we'll be right to say that at last we've reached an element, which cannot any longer be carried back to other names.

HERMOGENES: That seems right to me, at least.

SOCRATES: And if the names you're asking about now turn out to be elements, won't we have to investigate their correctness in a different manner from the one we've been using so far?

HERMOGENES: Probably so.

SOCRATES: It is certainly probable, Hermogenes. At any rate, it's obvious that all the earlier ones were resolved into these. So, if *c* they are indeed elements, as they seem to me to be, join me again in investigating them,[119] to ensure that I don't talk non-sense about the correctness of the first names.[120]

HERMOGENES: You have only to speak, and I will join in the in-vestigation so far as I'm able.

SOCRATES: I think you agree with me that there is only one kind of correctness in all names, primary as well as derivative, and that considered simply as names there is no difference between them.

HERMOGENES: Certainly.

d SOCRATES: Now, the correctness of every name we analyzed was intended to consist in its expressing the nature of one of the things that are.

---

118. See 412c.
119. See 393c.
120. *Ta prôta onomata*: Plato uses this phrase at 414c–d to refer to the first names given to things, whether or not they are elements. But here it seems to mean the names of elements only.

HERMOGENES: Of course.

SOCRATES: And this is no less true of primary names than derivative ones, if indeed they are names.

HERMOGENES: Certainly.

SOCRATES: But it seems that the derivative ones were able to accomplish this by means of the primary ones.

HERMOGENES: Apparently.

SOCRATES: Good. And if the primary names are indeed names, they must make the things that are as clear as possible to us. But how can they do this when they aren't based on other names? Answer me this: If we hadn't a voice or a tongue, and wanted to *e* express things to one another, wouldn't we try to make signs by moving our hands, head, and the rest of our body, just as dumb people do at present?

HERMOGENES: What other choice would we have, Socrates?

SOCRATES: So, if we wanted to express something light in weight or above us, I think we'd raise our hand towards the sky in imi- *423a* tation of the very nature of the thing. And if we wanted to express something heavy or below us, we'd move our hand towards the earth. And if we wanted to express a horse (or any other animal) galloping, you know that we'd make our bodies and our gestures as much like theirs as possible.

HERMOGENES: I think we'd have to.

SOCRATES: Because the only way to express anything by means of our body is to have our body imitate whatever we want to express.[121] *b*

HERMOGENES: Yes.

---

121. See *Republic* 394d ff.

SOCRATES: So, if we want to express a particular fact by using our voice, tongue, and mouth, we will succeed in doing so, if we succeed in imitating it by means of them?

HERMOGENES: That must be right, I think.

SOCRATES: It seems to follow that a name is a vocal imitation of what it imitates, and that someone who imitates something with his voice names what he imitates.

HERMOGENES: I think so.

SOCRATES: Well, *I* don't. I don't think this is a fine thing to say at
c   all.

HERMOGENES: Why not?

SOCRATES: Because then we'd have to agree that those who imitate sheep, cocks, or other animals are naming the things they imitate.

HERMOGENES: That's true, we would.

SOCRATES: And do you think that's a fine conclusion?

HERMOGENES: No, I don't. But then what sort of imitation is a name, Socrates?

SOCRATES: In the first place, if we imitate things the way we im-
d   itate them in music, we won't be naming them, not even if the imitation in question is vocal. And the same holds if we imitate the things music imitates. What I mean is this: each thing has a sound and a shape, and many of them have a color. Don't they?

HERMOGENES: Certainly.

SOCRATES: It doesn't seem to be the craft of naming that's concerned with imitating these qualities, however, but rather the crafts of music and painting. Isn't that so?

HERMOGENES: Yes.

SOCRATES: And what about this? Don't you think that just as   *e*
each thing has a color or some of those other qualities we mentioned, it also has a being or essence? Indeed, don't color and
sound each have a being or essence, just like every other thing
that we say "is"?

HERMOGENES: Yes, I think they do.

SOCRATES: So if someone were able to imitate in letters and syllables the being or essence that each thing has, wouldn't he express what each thing itself is?[122]

HERMOGENES: He certainly would.   *424a*

SOCRATES: And if you were to identify the person who is able to
do this, in just the way that you said the first was a musician and
the second a painter, what would you say he is?

HERMOGENES: I think he's the name-giver, Socrates, the one
we've been looking for from the beginning.

SOCRATES: If that's true, doesn't it seem that we are now in a position to investigate each of the names you were asking about[123]
—'rhoê' ('flowing'), 'ienai' ('going'), and 'schesis' ('restraining')—
to see whether or not he has grasped the being or essence of
each of the things they signify by imitating its being or essence
in the letters and syllables of its name. Isn't that so?   *b*

HERMOGENES: Certainly.

SOCRATES: Come, then, let's see if these are the only primary
names or if there are many others.

HERMOGENES: For my part, I think there are others.

---

122. See 389b.
123. See 421c.

SOCRATES: Yes, there probably are. But how are we to divide off the ones with which the imitator begins his imitation? Since an imitation of a thing's being or essence is made out of letters and syllables, wouldn't it be most correct for us to divide off the letters or elements first, just as those who set to work on speech

c rhythms first divide off the forces or powers of the letters or elements, then those of syllables, and only then investigate rhythms themselves?

HERMOGENES: Yes.

SOCRATES: So mustn't we first divide off the vowels and then the others in accordance with their differences in kind, that is to say, the "consonants" and "mutes" (as I take it they're called by specialists in these matters) and the semivowels, which are neither vowels nor mutes? And, as to the vowels themselves, mustn't we also divide off those that differ in kind from one another?[124] Then when we've also well divided off the things that are—the

d things to which we have to give names—if there are some things to which they can all be carried back, as names are to the letters, and from which we can see that they derive, and if different kinds of being are found among them, in just the way that there are among the letters[125]—once we've done all this well, we'll know how to apply each letter to what it resembles, whether one letter or a combination of many is to be applied to one thing. It's just the same as it is with painters. When they want to produce a resemblance, they sometimes use only purple, sometimes another color, and sometimes—for example, when they want to paint human flesh or something of that sort—they mix many colors, employing the particular color, I suppose, that their particular subject demands. Similarly, we'll apply letters to things, using one letter for one thing, when that's what seems to be required, or many letters together, to form what's called a syllable,

425a or many syllables combined to form names and verbs. From names and verbs, in turn, we shall finally construct something important, beautiful, and whole. And just as the painter painted

---

124. See *Philebus* 18b–d.
125. See 386e ff.

an animal, so—by means of the craft of naming or rhetoric or whatever it is—we shall construct sentences. Of course, I don't really mean *we ourselves*—I was carried away by the discussion. It was *the ancients* who combined things in this way. Our job—if indeed we are to examine all these things with scientific knowledge—is to divide where they put together, so as to see whether or not both the primary and derivative names are given in accord with nature. Any other way of connecting names together, Hermogenes, will be inferior and unsystematic.   *b*

HERMOGENES: By god, Socrates, it probably would.

SOCRATES: Well, then, do you think you could divide them in that way? I don't think I could.

HERMOGENES: Then it's even less likely that I could.

SOCRATES: Shall we give up then? Or do you want us to do what we can, and try to see a little of what these names are like? Aren't we in a similar situation to the one we were in a while ago with the gods?[126] We prefaced that discussion by saying that   *c* we were wholly ignorant of the truth, and were merely describing human beliefs about the gods. So, shouldn't we now say this to ourselves[127] before we proceed: if anyone, whether ourselves or someone else, divides names scientifically,[128] he will divide them in the way we have just described, but, given our present situation, we must follow the proverb and "do the best we can"[129] to work at them? Do you agree or not?

HERMOGENES: Of course, I agree completely.

SOCRATES: Perhaps it will seem absurd, Hermogenes, to think   *d* that things become clear by being imitated in letters and syllables, but it is absolutely unavoidable. For we have nothing bet-

---

126. See 401a.
127. Reading *hêmin* with Duke et al.
128. Reading *technikôs* with Duke et al.
129. See *Hippias Major* 301c.

ter on which to base the truth of primary names. Unless you want us to behave like tragic poets, who introduce a *deus ex machina* whenever they're perplexed. For we, too, could escape our difficulties by saying that the primary names are correct because they were given by the gods. But is that the best account

e we can give? Or is it this one: that we got them from foreigners, who are more ancient[130] than we are? Or this: that just as it is impossible to investigate foreign names,[131] so it is impossible to investigate the primary ones because they are too ancient? Aren't

426a all these merely the clever excuses of people who have no account to offer of how primary names are correctly given? And yet regardless of what kind of excuse one offers, if one doesn't know about the correctness of primary names, one cannot know about the correctness of derivative ones, which can only express something by means of those others about which one knows nothing. Clearly, then, anyone who claims to have a scientific understanding of derivative names must first and foremost be

b able to explain the primary ones with perfect clarity. Otherwise he can be certain that what he says about the others will be worthless. Or do you disagree?

HERMOGENES: No, Socrates, not in the least.

SOCRATES: Well, my impressions about primary names seem to me to be entirely outrageous and absurd. Nonetheless, I'll share them with you, if you like. But if you have something better to offer, I hope you'll share it with me.

HERMOGENES: I will. But you have courage and speak.

c SOCRATES: First off, '*r*' seems to me to be a tool for copying every sort of motion (*kinêsis*).—We haven't said why motion has this

---

130. '*Archaioteros*': the comparative of '*archaios*'. It literally means 'older' or 'more ancient', but its connection to '*archê*' ('origin' or 'first principle') suggests that Plato is saying this: "that we got them from foreigners, who, being more ancient than we are, have more insight into first principles than we do."
131. See 409d ff.

name, but it's clear that it means *'hesis'* ('a going forth'), since in ancient times we used *'e'* in place of *'ê'*. The first part comes from *'kiein'*, a non-Attic name equivalent to *'ienai'* ('moving'). So if you wanted to find an ancient name corresponding to the present *'kinêsis'*, the correct answer would be *'hesis'*. But nowadays, what with the non-Attic word *'kiein'*, the change from *'e'* to *'ê'*, and the insertion of *'n'*, we say *'kinêsis'*, though it ought to be *'kieiesis'* or *'kiesis'*.[132] *'Stasis'* ('rest') is a beautified version of *'staesis'*,[133] which means the opposite of *'ienai'* ('moving').—In any case, as I was saying, the letter *'r'* seemed to the name-giver to be a beautiful tool for copying motion, at any rate he often uses it for this purpose. He first uses this letter to imitate motion in the names *'rhein'* ('flowing') and *'rhoê'* ('flow') themselves. Then in *'tromos'* ('trembling') and *'trechein'* ('running'), and in such verbs as *'krouein'* ('striking'), *'thrauein'* ('crushing'), *'ereikein'* ('rending'), *'thruptein'* ('breaking'), *'kermatizein'* ('crumbling'), *'rhumbein'* ('whirling'), it is mostly *'r'* he uses to imitate these motions. He saw, I suppose, that the tongue was most agitated and least at rest in pronouncing this letter, and that's probably why he used it in these names. He uses *'i'*, in turn, to imitate all the small things that can most easily penetrate everything.[134] Hence, in *'ienai'* ('moving') and *'hiesthai'* ('hastening'), he uses *'i'* to do the imitating. Similarly, he uses *'phi'*, *'psi'*, *'s'*, and *'z'* to do the imitating in such names as *'psuchron'* ('chilling'), *'zeon'* ('seething'), *'seiesthai'* ('shaking'), and *'seismos'* ('quaking'), because all these letters are pronounced with an expulsion of breath. Indeed, whenever the name-giver wants to imitate some sort of blowing or hard breathing (*phusôdes*), he almost always seems to employ them. He also seems to have thought that the compression and stopping of the power of the tongue involved in pronouncing *'d'* and *'t'* made such names as *'desmos'* ('shackling') and *'stasis'* ('rest') appropriately imitative. And because he observed that the tongue glides most of all in pronouncing *'l'*, he uses it to produce a resemblance in *'oligisthanein'* ('glide') itself, and in such names as *'leion'*

d

e

427a

b

---

132. Reading *'kieiesin'* or *'kiesin'* with Duke et al.
133. Reading *staesis* at 426d1 with Duke et al.
134. See 412d ff.

('smooth'), *'liparon'* ('sleek'), *'kollôdes'* ('viscous'), and the like. But when he wants to imitate something cloying, he uses names, such as *'glischron'* ('gluey'), *'gluku'* ('sweet'), and *'gloiôdes'* ('clammy'), in which the gliding of the tongue is stopped by the power of the *'g'*. And because he saw that *'n'* is sounded in-
c   wardly, he used it in *'endon'* ('within') and *'entos'* ('inside'), in order to make the letters copy the things. He put an *'a'* in *'mega'* ('large') and an *'ê'* in *'mêkos'* ('length') because these letters are both pronounced long. He wanted *'o'* to signify roundness, so he mixed lots of it into the name *'goggulon'* ('round'). In the same way, the rule-setter apparently used the other letters or elements as likenesses in order to make a sign or name for each of the things that are, and then compounded all the remaining names out of these, imitating the things they name. That, Hermogenes,
d   is my view of what it means to say that names are correct—un-
less, of course, Cratylus disagrees.

HERMOGENES: Well, Socrates, as I said at the beginning, Cratylus confuses me a lot of the time. He *says* that there is such a thing as the correctness of names, but he never explains clearly what it is. Consequently, I'm never able to determine whether his lack of clarity is intentional or unintentional. So tell me now, Cratylus,
e   here in the presence of Socrates, do you agree with what he has been saying about names, or do you have something better to say? If you have, tell it to us, and either you'll learn about your errors from Socrates or become our teacher.

CRATYLUS: But, Hermogenes, do you really think that any sub-ject can be taught or learned so quickly, not to mention one like this, which seems to be among the most important?

428a   HERMOGENES: No, by god, I don't. But I think that Hesiod is right in saying that

If you can add even a little to a little, it's worthwhile.[135]

---

135. *Works and Days*, 359.

So, if you can add even a little more, don't shrink from the labor, but assist Socrates—he deserves it—and assist me, too.

SOCRATES: Yes, Cratylus, please do. As far as I'm concerned, nothing I've said is set in stone. I have simply been saying what seems right to me as a result of my investigations with Hermogenes. So, don't hesitate to speak, and if your views are better than mine, I'll gladly accept them. And it wouldn't surprise me   *b* if they were better, for you've both investigated these matters for yourself and learned about them from others. So, if indeed you do happen to have something better to offer, you may sign me up as a student in your course on the correctness of names.

CRATYLUS: Yes, Socrates, I have, as you say, occupied myself with these matters, and it's possible that you might have something to learn from me. But I fear the opposite is altogether more likely. So much so, indeed, that it occurs to me to say to you   *c* what Achilles says to Ajax in the "Prayers":

Ajax, son of Telamon, seed of Zeus, lord of the people,
All you have said to me seems spoken after my own mind.[136]

The same is true of me where you're concerned, Socrates: your oracular utterances—whether inspired by Euthyphro or by some other Muse who has long inhabited your own mind without your knowing about it—seem to be pretty much spoken after *my* own mind.

SOCRATES: But, Cratylus, *I* have long been surprised at my own   *d* wisdom—and doubtful of it, too.[137] That's why I think it's necessary to keep re-investigating whatever I say, since self-deception is the worst thing of all. How could it not be terrible, indeed, when the deceiver never deserts you even for an instant but is always right there with you? Therefore, I think we have to turn

---

136. *Iliad* 9.644–5. "Prayers": the *Iliad* and *Odyssey* were not divided into the now familiar twenty-four books when Plato was writing, so passages were identified episodically.
137. See *Apology* 21b ff.

back frequently to what we've already said, in order to test it by looking at it "backwards and forwards simultaneously," as the aforementioned poet puts it.[138] So, let's now see what we *have* said. We said that the correctness of a name consists in display-
e   ing the nature of the thing it names. And is that statement satis-factory?

CRATYLUS: In my view, Socrates, it is entirely satisfactory.

SOCRATES: So names are spoken in order to give instruction?

CRATYLUS: Certainly.

SOCRATES: Is there a craft for that and are there craftsmen who practice it?

CRATYLUS: Certainly.

SOCRATES: Who are they?

CRATYLUS: As you said at the beginning, they're the rule-
429a   setters.[139]

SOCRATES: Is this craft attributed to human beings in the same way as other crafts or not? What I mean is this: aren't some painters better or worse than others?

CRATYLUS: Certainly.

SOCRATES: And the better painters produce finer products or paintings, while the others produce inferior ones? Similarly with builders—some build finer houses, others build inferior ones?

CRATYLUS: Yes.

---

138. *Iliad* 1.343.
139. See 388d ff.

SOCRATES: What about rule-setters? Do some of them produce finer products, others inferior ones?   *b*

CRATYLUS: No, there I no longer agree with you.

SOCRATES: So you don't think that some rules are better, others inferior?

CRATYLUS: Certainly not.

SOCRATES: Nor names either, it seems. Or do you think that some names have been better given, others worse?

CRATYLUS: Certainly not.

SOCRATES: So all names have been correctly given?

CRATYLUS: Yes, as many of them as are names at all.

SOCRATES: What about the case of Hermogenes, which we mentioned earlier? Has he not been given this name at all, unless he belongs to the family of Hermes? Or has he been given it, only   *c* not correctly?

CRATYLUS: I think he hasn't been given it at all, Socrates. People take it to have been given to him, but it is really the name of someone else, namely, the very one who also has the nature.

SOCRATES: What about when someone says that our friend here is Hermogenes? Is he speaking falsely or is he not even managing to do that much? Is it even possible to say that he *is* Hermogenes, if he isn't?

CRATYLUS: What do you mean?

SOCRATES: That false speaking is in every way impossible, for   *d* isn't that what *you* are trying to say? Certainly, many people do say it nowadays, Cratylus, and many have said it in the past as well.

CRATYLUS: But, Socrates, how can anyone say the thing he says and not say something that is? Doesn't speaking falsely consist in not saying things that are?

SOCRATES: Your argument is too subtle for me at my age. All the same, tell me this. Do you think it is possible to say something *e* falsely, although not possible to speak it falsely?

CRATYLUS: In my view, one can neither speak nor say anything falsely.

SOCRATES: What about announcing something falsely or addressing someone falsely? For example, suppose you were in a foreign country and someone meeting you took your hand and said, "Greetings! Hermogenes, son of Smicrion, visitor from Athens," would he be speaking, saying, announcing, or addressing these words not to you but to Hermogenes—or to no one?

CRATYLUS: In my view, Socrates, he is not articulating them as he should.

SOCRATES: Well, that's a welcome answer. But are the words he *430a* articulates true or false, or partly true and partly false? If you tell me that, I'll be satisfied.

CRATYLUS: For my part, I'd say he's just making noise and acting pointlessly, as if he were banging a brass pot.

SOCRATES: Let's see, Cratylus, if we can somehow come to terms with one another. You agree, don't you, that it's one thing to be a name and another to be the thing it names?

CRATYLUS: Yes, I do.

SOCRATES: And you also agree that a name is an imitation of a *b* thing?

CRATYLUS: Absolutely.

SOCRATES: And that a painting is a different sort of imitation of a thing?

CRATYLUS: Yes.

SOCRATES: Well, perhaps what you're saying is correct and I'm misunderstanding you, but can both of these imitations—both paintings and names—be assigned and applied to the things of which they are imitations, or not?

CRATYLUS: They can.   *c*

SOCRATES: Then consider this. Can we assign a likeness of a man to a man and that of a woman to a woman, and so on?

CRATYLUS: Certainly.

SOCRATES: What about the opposite? Can we assign the likeness of a man to a woman and that of a woman to a man?

CRATYLUS: Yes, we can.

SOCRATES: And are both these assignments correct, or only the first?

CRATYLUS: Only the first.

SOCRATES: That is to say, the one that assigns to each thing the painting or name that is appropriate to it or like it?

CRATYLUS: That's my view, at least.

SOCRATES: Since you and I are friends, we don't want to engage in a battle of words, so here's what I think. I call the first kind of   *d* assignment correct, whether it's an assignment of a painting or a name, but if it's an assignment of a name, I call it both correct and *true*. And I call the other kind of assignment, the one that assigns and applies unlike imitations, incorrect, and, in the case of names, *false* as well.

CRATYLUS: But it may be, Socrates, that it's possible to assign
e   paintings incorrectly, but not names, which must always be correctly assigned.

SOCRATES: What do you mean? What's the difference between
them? Can't I step up to a man and say "This is your portrait,"
while showing him what happens to be his own likeness, or
what happens to be the likeness of a woman? And by "show" I
mean bring before the sense of sight.

CRATYLUS: Certainly.

SOCRATES: Well, then, can't I step up to the same man a second
time and say, "This is your name"? Now, a name is an imitation,
just as a painting or portrait is. So, can't I say to him, "This is
431a   your name," and after that put before his sense of hearing
what happens to be an imitation of himself, saying "Man,"
or what happens to be an imitation of a female of the human
species, saying "Woman"? Don't you think that all this is possible and sometimes occurs?

CRATYLUS: I'm willing to go along with you, Socrates, and say
that it occurs.

SOCRATES: It's good of you to do so, Cratylus, if it does occur,
since then we don't have to argue any further about the matter.
So if some such assignments occur in the case of names, we may
b   call the first of them speaking truly and the second speaking
falsely. But if that is so, it is sometimes possible to assign names
incorrectly, to give them not to things they fit but to things they
don't fit. The same is true of verbs. But if verbs and names can
be assigned in this way, the same must be true of statements,
since statements are, I believe, a combination of names and
c   verbs. What do you think, Cratylus?

CRATYLUS: The same as you, since I think you're right.

SOCRATES: Further, primary names may be compared to paintings, and in paintings it's possible to present all the appropriate
colors and shapes, or not to present them all. Some may be left

out, or too many included, or those included may be too large.
Isn't that so?

CRATYLUS: It is.

SOCRATES: So doesn't someone who presents all of them, present
a fine painting or likeness, while someone who adds some or
leaves some out, though he still produces a painting or likeness,
produces a bad one?

CRATYLUS: Yes.   *d*

SOCRATES: What about someone who imitates the being or
essence of things in syllables and letters? According to this account, if he presents all the appropriate things, won't the likeness—that is to say, the name—be a fine one? But if he happens
to add a little or leave a little out, though he'll still have pro-
duced an image, it won't be fine? Doesn't it follow that some
names are finely made, while others are made badly?

CRATYLUS: Presumably.

SOCRATES: So presumably one person will be a good craftsman
of names and another a bad one?   *e*

CRATYLUS: Yes.

SOCRATES: And this craftsman is named a rule-setter.

CRATYLUS: Yes.

SOCRATES: By god, presumably some rule-setters are good and
others bad then, especially if what we agreed to before is true,
and they are just like other craftsmen.

CRATYLUS: That's right. But you see, Socrates, when we assign
'*a*', '*b*', and each of the other letters to names by using the craft of
grammar, if we add, subtract, or transpose a letter, we don't simply write the name incorrectly, we don't write *it* at all, for it im-   *432a*
mediately becomes a different name, if any of those things happens.

SOCRATES: That's not a good way for us to look at the matter, Cratylus.

CRATYLUS: Why not?

SOCRATES: What you say may well be true of numbers, which have to be a certain number or not be at all. For example, if you add anything to the number ten or subtract anything from it, it immediately becomes a different number, and the same is true of any other number you choose. But this isn't the sort of cor-
b   rectness that belongs to things with sensory qualities, and to images in general. Indeed, the opposite is true of them—an image cannot remain an image if it presents all the details of what it represents. See if I'm right. Would there be two things— Cratylus and an image of Cratylus—in the following circumstances? Suppose some god didn't just represent your color and shape the way painters do, but made all the inner parts like yours, with the same warmth and softness, and put motion,
c   soul, and wisdom like yours into them—in a word, suppose he made a duplicate of everything you have and put it beside you. Would there then be two Cratyluses or Cratylus and an image of Cratylus?

CRATYLUS: It seems to me, Socrates, that there would be two Cratyluses.

SOCRATES: So don't you see that we must look for some other kind of correctness in images and in the names we've been discussing, and not insist that if a detail is added to an image or omitted from it, it's no longer an image at all. Or haven't you no-
d   ticed how far images are from having the same features as the things of which they are images?

CRATYLUS: Yes, I have.

SOCRATES: At any rate, Cratylus, names would have an absurd effect on the things they name, if they resembled them in every respect, since all of them would then be duplicated, and no one would be able to say which was the thing and which was the name.

CRATYLUS: That's true.

SOCRATES: Take courage then and admit that one name may be well given while another isn't. Don't insist that it have all the letters and exactly resemble the thing it names, but allow that an   *e* inappropriate letter may be included. But if an inappropriate letter may be included in a name, an inappropriate name may be included in a phrase. And if an inappropriate name may be included in a phrase, a phrase which is inappropriate to the things may be employed in a statement. Things are still named and described when this happens, provided the phrases include the pattern of the things they're about. Remember that this is just what Hermogenes and I claimed earlier about the names of the elements.[140]   *433a*

CRATYLUS: I remember.

SOCRATES: Good. So even if a name doesn't include all the appropriate letters, it will still describe the thing if it includes its pattern—though it will describe the thing well, if it includes all the appropriate letters, and badly, if it includes few of them. I think we had better accept this, Cratylus, or else, like men lost on the streets of Aegina late at night,[141] we, too, may incur the charge of truly seeming to be the sort of people who arrive at things later than they should. For if you deny it, you cannot agree that a name is correct if it expresses things by means of let-   *b* ters and syllables and you'll have to search for some other account of the correctness of names, since if you both deny it and accept this account of correctness, you'll contradict yourself.

CRATYLUS: You seem to me to be speaking reasonably, Socrates, and I take what you've said as established.

SOCRATES: Well, then, since we agree about that, let's consider

---

140. See 393d–e.
141. This may be a reference to some particular story or proverb, or it may be that the streets of Aegina were notoriously difficult to negotiate.

the next point. If a name is well given, don't we say that it must have the appropriate letters?

CRATYLUS: Yes.

SOCRATES: And the appropriate letters are the ones that are like
c   the things?

CRATYLUS: Certainly.

SOCRATES: Therefore that's the way that well-given names are given. But if a name isn't well given, it's probable that most of its letters are appropriate or like the thing it names, if indeed it is a likeness of it, but that some are inappropriate and prevent the name from being good or well given. Is that our view or is it something different?

CRATYLUS: I don't suppose there's anything to be gained by continuing to quarrel, Socrates, but I'm not satisfied that something is a name if it isn't well given.

d   SOCRATES: But you *are* satisfied that a name is a way of expressing a thing?

CRATYLUS: I am.

SOCRATES: And you think it's true that some names are composed out of more primitive ones, while others are primary?

CRATYLUS: Yes, I do.

SOCRATES: But if the primary names are to be ways of expressing things clearly, is there any better way of getting them to be such
e   than by making each of them as much like the thing it is to express as possible? Or do you prefer the way proposed by Hermogenes and many others, who claim that names are conventional signs that express things to those who already knew the things before they established the conventions? Do you think that the correctness of names is conventional, so that it makes no difference whether we accept the present convention or adopt

the opposite one, calling 'big' what we now call 'small', and 'small' what we now call 'big'? Which of these two ways of getting names to express things do you prefer?

CRATYLUS: A name that expresses a thing by being like it is in every way superior, Socrates, to one that is given by chance. *434a*

SOCRATES: That's right. But if a name is indeed to be like a thing, mustn't the letters or elements out of which primary names are composed be naturally like things? Let me explain by returning to our earlier analogy with painting.[142] Could a painting ever be made like any of the things that are, if it were not composed of pigments that were by nature like the things that the art of *b* painting imitates? Isn't that impossible?

CRATYLUS: Yes, it's impossible.

SOCRATES: Then by the same token can names ever be like anything unless the things they're composed out of first have some kind of likeness to the things they imitate? And aren't they composed of letters or elements?

CRATYLUS: Yes.

SOCRATES: Now, consider what I said to Hermogenes earlier. Tell me, do you think I was right to say that '*r*' is like motion, mov- *c* ing, and hardness or not?[143]

CRATYLUS: You were right.

SOCRATES: And '*l*' is like smoothness, softness, and the other things we mentioned.[144]

CRATYLUS: Yes.

---

142. See 430b ff., and 424d–425a.
143. See 426c–e.
144. See 427b.

SOCRATES: Yet you know that the very thing that we call *'sklêrotês'* ('hardness') is called *'sklêrotêr'* by the Eretrians?

CRATYLUS: Certainly.

SOCRATES: Then are both *'r'* and *'s'* like the same thing, and does the name ending in *'r'* express the same thing to them as the one ending in *'s'* does to us, or does one of them fail to express it?

d   CRATYLUS: They both express it.

SOCRATES: In so far as *'r'* and *'s'* are alike, or in so far as they are unlike?

CRATYLUS: In so far as they are alike.

SOCRATES: Are they alike in all respects?

CRATYLUS: They are presumably alike with respect to expressing motion, at any rate.

SOCRATES: What about the *'l'* in these names? Doesn't it express the opposite of hardness?

CRATYLUS: Perhaps it is incorrectly included in them, Socrates. Maybe it's just like the examples you cited to Hermogenes a while ago in which you added or subtracted letters. You were correct to do so, in my view. So, too, in the present case perhaps we ought to replace *'l'* with *'r'*.

SOCRATES: You have a point. But what about when someone says *'sklêron'* ('hard'), and pronounces it the way we do at
e   present? Don't we understand him? Don't you yourself know what *I* mean by it?

CRATYLUS: I do, but that's because of usage.

SOCRATES: When you say 'usage', do you mean something other than convention? Do you mean something by 'usage' besides this: when I utter this name and mean hardness by it, you know that this is what I mean? Isn't that what you're saying?

CRATYLUS: Yes.   435a

SOCRATES: And if when I utter a name, you know what I mean, doesn't that name become a way for me to express it to you?

CRATYLUS: Yes.

SOCRATES: Even though the name I utter is unlike the thing I mean—since 'l' is unlike hardness (to revert to your example). But if that's right, surely you have entered into a convention with yourself, and the correctness of names has become a matter of convention for you, for isn't it the chance of usage and convention that makes both like and unlike letters express things? And even if usage is completely different from convention, still you must say that expressing something isn't a matter of likeness but of usage, since usage, it seems, enables both like and   b
unlike names to express things. Since we agree on these points, Cratylus, for I take your silence as a sign of agreement, both convention and usage must contribute something to expressing what we mean when we speak. Consider numbers, Cratylus, since you want to have recourse to them.[145] Where do you think you'll get names that are like each one of the numbers, if you don't allow this agreement and convention of yours to have some control over the correctness of names? I myself prefer the   c
view that names should be as much like things as possible, but I fear that defending this view is like hauling a ship up a sticky ramp, as Hermogenes suggested,[146] and that we have to make use of this worthless thing, convention, in the correctness of names. For probably the best possible way to speak consists in using names all (or most) of which are like the things they name (that is, are appropriate to them[147]), while the worst is to use the opposite kind of names. But let me next ask you this. What   d
power do names have for us? What's the good of them?

                                                                    9/12

---

145. See 432a.
146. At 414c.
147. See 430c.

CRATYLUS: To give instruction, Socrates. After all, the simple truth is that anyone who knows a thing's name also knows the thing.

SOCRATES: Perhaps you mean this, Cratylus, that when you know what a name is like, and it is like the thing it names, then

e   you also know the thing, since it is like the name, and all like things fall under one and the same craft. Isn't that why you say that whoever knows a thing's name also knows the thing?

CRATYLUS: Yes, you're absolutely right.

SOCRATES: Then let's look at that way of giving instruction about the things that are. Is there also another one, but inferior to this, or is it the only one? What do you think?

CRATYLUS: I think that it is the best and only way, and that there

436*a*   are no others.

SOCRATES: Is it also the best way to *discover* the things that are? If one discovers something's name has one also discovered the thing it names? Or are names only a way of getting people to learn things, and must investigation and discovery be undertaken in some different way?

CRATYLUS: They must certainly be undertaken in exactly the same way and by means of the same things.

SOCRATES: But don't you see, Cratylus, that anyone who investigates things by taking names as his guides and looking into

b   their meanings runs no small risk of being deceived?

CRATYLUS: In what way?

SOCRATES: It's clear that the first name-giver gave names to things based on his conception of what those things were like.[148] Isn't that right?

---

148. See 401b.

CRATYLUS: Yes.

SOCRATES: And if his conception was incorrect and he gave names based on it, what do you suppose will happen to us if we take him as our guide? Won't we be deceived?

CRATYLUS: But it wasn't that way, Socrates. The name-giver had to know the things he was naming. Otherwise, as I've been say-   c
ing all along, his names wouldn't be names at all. And here's a powerful proof for you that the name-giver didn't miss the truth: His names are entirely consistent with one another. Or haven't you noticed that all the names you utter are based on the same assumption[149] and have the same purpose?

SOCRATES: But surely that's no defense, Cratylus. The name-giver might have made a mistake at the beginning and then forced the other names to be consistent with it. There would be   d
nothing strange in that. It is just that way sometimes in geometrical constructions: given the initial error, small and unnoticed, all the rest that then follow are perfectly consistent with one another. That's why every man must think a lot about the first principles of anything and investigate them thoroughly to see whether or not it's correct to assume them.[150] For if they have been adequately examined, the subsequent steps will plainly follow from them. However, I'd be surprised if names *are* actually   e
consistent with one another. So let's review our earlier discussion. We said that names signify the being or essence of things to us on the assumption that all things are moving and flowing and being swept along. Isn't that what you think names express?

CRATYLUS: Absolutely. Moreover, I think they signify correctly.   437a

SOCRATES: Of those we discussed, let's reconsider the name 'epistêmê' ('knowledge') first and see how ambiguous it is. It seems to signify that it stops (*histêsi*) the movement of our soul towards (*epi*) things, rather than that it accompanies them in

---

149. See 411c where Socrates himself suggests such a principle.
150. See *Republic* 377a–b, 510c–511d.

their movement, so that it's more correct to pronounce the beginning of it as we now do than to insert an *'h'* and get *'hepistêmê'*[151]—or rather, to insert it before the *'i'* instead of the *'e'*.[152] Next, consider *'bebaion'* ('certain'), which is an imitation of being based (*basis*) or resting (*stasis*), not of motion. *'Historia'* ('inquiry'), which is somewhat the same, signifies the stopping

b   (*histêsi*) of the flow (*rhous*). *'Piston'* ('confidence'), too, certainly signifies stopping (*histan*). Next, anyone can see that *'mnêmê'* ('memory') means a staying (*monê*) in the soul, not a motion. Or consider *'hamartia'* ('error') and *'sumphora'* ('mishap'), if you like. If we take names as our guides, they seem to signify the same as *'sunesis'* ('comprehension') and *'epistêmê'* ('knowledge') and other names of excellent things.[153] Moreover, *'amathia'* ('ignorance') and *'akolasia'* ('licentiousness') also seem to be closely akin to them. For *'amathia'* seems to mean the journey of some-

c   one who accompanies god (*hama theô(i) iôn*), and *'akolasia'* seems precisely to mean movement guided by things (*akolouthia tois pragmasin*). Thus names of what we consider to be the very worst things seem to be exactly like those of the very best. And if one took the trouble, I think one could find many other names from which one could conclude that the name-giver intended to signify not that things were moving and being swept along, but the opposite, that they were at rest.

CRATYLUS: But observe, Socrates, that most of them signify

d   motion.

SOCRATES: What if they do, Cratylus? Are we to count names like votes and determine their correctness that way? If more names signify motion, does that make *them* the true ones?

CRATYLUS: No, that's not a reasonable view.

---

151. Reading *'hepistêmê'* with Duke et al. See 412a.
152. To get *'ephistêmê'* from *'epi'* and *'histêsi'*. As suggested to me by David Sedley and to him by Malcolm Schofield.
153. *'Hamartia'* is like *'homartein'* ('to accompany'), and *'sumphora'* is like *'sumpheresthai'* ('to move together with').

SOCRATES: It certainly isn't, Cratylus. So let's drop this topic, and return to the one that led us here. A little while ago, you *438a* said, if you remember, that the name-giver had to know the things he named.[154] Do you still believe that or not?

CRATYLUS: I still do.

SOCRATES: Do you think that the giver of the first names also knew the things he named?

CRATYLUS: Yes, he did know them.

SOCRATES: What names did he learn or discover those things from? After all, the first names had not yet been given. Yet it's *b* impossible, on our view, to learn or discover things except by learning their names from others or discovering them for ourselves?

CRATYLUS: You have a point there, Socrates.

SOCRATES: So, if things cannot be learned except from their names, how can we possibly claim that the name-givers or rule-setters had knowledge before any names had been given for them to know?

CRATYLUS: I think the truest account of the matter, Socrates, is *c* that a more than human power gave the first names to things, so that they are necessarily correct.[155]

SOCRATES: In your view then this name-giver contradicted himself, even though he's either a daimon or a god? Or do you think we were talking nonsense just now?[156]

CRATYLUS: But one of the two apparently contradictory groups of names that we distinguished aren't names at all.

---

154. See 436b.
155. See 425d–426a.
156. See 437a ff.

SOCRATES: Which one, Cratylus? Those which point to rest or those which point to motion? As we said just now, this cannot be settled by majority vote.

d   CRATYLUS: No, that wouldn't be right, Socrates.

SOCRATES: But since there's a civil war among names, with some claiming that they are like the truth and others claiming that *they* are, how then are we to judge between them, and what are we to start from? We can't start from other different names because there are none. No, it's clear we'll have to look for something other than names, something that will make plain to us without using names which of these two kinds of names are the true ones—that is to say, the ones that express the truth about
e   the things that are.

CRATYLUS: I think so, too.

SOCRATES: But if that's right, Cratylus, then it seems it must be possible to learn about the things that are, independently of names.

CRATYLUS: Evidently.

SOCRATES: How else would you expect to learn about them? How else than in the most legitimate and natural way, namely, learning them through one another, if they are somehow akin,[157] and through themselves? For something different, something that was other than they, wouldn't signify them, but something different, something other.

CRATYLUS: That seems true to me.

SOCRATES: But wait a minute! Haven't we often agreed that if
439a names are well given, they are like the things they name and so are likenesses of them?

---

157. See *Meno* 81c ff.

CRATYLUS: Yes.

SOCRATES: So if it's really the case that one can learn about things through names and that one can also learn about them through themselves, which would be the better and clearer way to learn about them? Is it better to learn from the likeness both whether it itself is a good likeness and also the truth it is a likeness of? Or is it better to learn from the truth both the truth itself and also whether the likeness of it is properly made?   *b*

CRATYLUS: I think it is certainly better to learn from the truth.

SOCRATES: How to learn and make discoveries about the things that are is probably too large a topic for you or me. But we should be content to have agreed that it is far better to investigate them and learn about them through themselves than to do so through their names.

CRATYLUS: Evidently so, Socrates.

SOCRATES: Still, let's investigate one further issue so as to avoid being deceived by the fact that so many of these names seem to lean in the same direction—as we will be if, as seems to me to be   *c* the case, the name-givers really did give them in the belief that everything is always moving and flowing, and as it happens things aren't really that way at all, but the name-givers themselves have fallen into a kind of vortex and are whirled around in it, dragging us with them.[158] Consider, Cratylus, a question that I for my part often dream about: Are we or aren't we to say that there is a beautiful itself, and a good itself, and the same for each one of the things that are?   *d*

CRATYLUS: I think we are, Socrates.

SOCRATES: Let's not investigate whether a particular face or something of that sort is beautiful then, or whether all such things seem to be flowing, but let's ask this instead: Are we to say that the beautiful itself is always such as it is?

---

158. See 411b.

CRATYLUS: Absolutely.

SOCRATES: But if it is always passing away, can we correctly say of it first that it is *this*, and then that it is *such and such*?[159] Or, at the very instant we are speaking, isn't it inevitably and immediately becoming a different thing and altering and no longer being as it was?

CRATYLUS: It is.

SOCRATES: Then if it never stays the same, how can it *be* something?[160] After all, if it ever stays the same, it clearly isn't changing—at least, not during that time; and if it always stays the same and is always the same thing, so that it never departs from its own form, how can it ever change or move?

e

CRATYLUS: There's no way.

SOCRATES: Then again it can't even be known by anyone. For at the very instant the knower-to-be approaches, what he is approaching is becoming a different thing, of a different character, so that he can't yet come to know either what sort of thing it is or what it is like—surely, no kind of knowledge is knowledge of what isn't in any way.[161]

440a

CRATYLUS: That's right.

SOCRATES: Indeed, it isn't even reasonable to say that there is such a thing as knowledge, Cratylus, if all things are passing on and none remain. For if that thing itself, knowledge, did not pass on from being knowledge, then knowledge would always remain, and there would *be* such a thing as knowledge. On the other hand, if the very form of knowledge passed on from being

---

159. When we say "the beautiful itself is always flowing," we first identify it as a *this* ("the beautiful itself"), then characterize it as such and such ("always flowing").
160. See *Timaeus* 49d–50b.
161. See *Republic* 477a.

knowledge, the instant it passed on into a different form than   *b*
that of knowledge, there would be no knowledge. And if it were
always passing on, there would always be no knowledge.
Hence, on this account, no one could know anything and nothing could be known either. But if there is always that which
knows and that which is known, if there are such things as the
beautiful, the good, and each one of the things that are, it
doesn't appear to me that these things can be at all like flowings
or motions, as we were saying just now they were. So whether
I'm right about these things or whether the truth lies with Hera-   *c*
clitus and many others isn't an easy matter to investigate. But
surely no one with any understanding will commit himself or
the cultivation of his soul to names, or trust them and their
givers to the point of firmly stating that he knows something,
nor will he condemn both himself and the things that are as totally unsound and all flowing like leaky pots, or believe that
things are exactly like people with runny noses, or that all things   *d*
are afflicted with colds and drip over everything. It's certainly
possible that things are that way, Cratylus, but it is also possible
that they are not. So you must investigate them courageously
and thoroughly and not accept anything easily—you are still
young and in your prime, after all. Then after you've investigated them, if you happen to discover the truth, you can share it
with me.

CRATYLUS: I'll do that. But I assure you, Socrates, that I have already investigated them and have taken a lot of trouble over the
matter, and things seem to me to be very much more as Heracli-   *e*
tus says they are.

SOCRATES: Instruct me about it another time, Cratylus, after you
get back. But now go off into the country, as you were planning
to do, and Hermogenes here will see you on your way.[162]

CRATYLUS: I'll do that, Socrates, but I hope that you will also
continue to think about these matters yourself.

162. *Propempsei*: See Introduction, p. liii.

SELECT BIBLIOGRAPHY

Text, Translations, Commentaries

Aronadio, F. *Platone Cratilo* (Bari, 1996).

Burnet, J. *Platonis Opera* I (Oxford, 1900).

Dalimier, C. *Platon Cratyle* (Paris, 1997).

Duke, E. A. et al. *Platonis Opera* I (Oxford, 1995).

Fowler, H. N. *Plato: Cratylus, Parmenides, Greater and Lesser Hippias* (Cambridge, 1926).

Gatti, M. L. *Platone Cratilo*, in *Tutti gli Scritti* (Milan, 1991).

Jowett, B. *Cratylus*, in E. Hamilton and H. Cairns (eds.), *Plato Collected Dialogues* (New York, 1966).

Méridier, L. *Platon Cratyle* (Paris, 1931).

Proclus, D. *In Platonis Cratylum Commentaria* (Leipzig, 1908).

Rijlaarsdam, J. C. *Platon über die Sprache, ein Kommentar zum Kratylos* (Utrecht, 1978).

Robin, L. *Platon Cratyle* in *Oeuvres Complète* Vol. 1 (Paris, 1950).

Works on the *Cratylus*

Ackrill, J. L. "Language and Reality in Plato's *Cratylus*." In his *Essays on Plato and Aristotle* (Oxford, 1997), 33–52.

Allan, D. J. "The Problem of Cratylus." *American Journal of Philology* 75 (1954), 271–87.

Anagnostopoulos, G. "Plato's *Cratylus*: The Two Theories of the Correctness of Names." *Review of Metaphysics* 25 (1971/2), 691–736.

———. "The Significance of Plato's *Cratylus*." *Review of Metaphysics* 27 (1973/4), 318–45.

Annas, J. "Knowledge and Language: the *Theaetetus* and the *Cratylus*." In M. Schofield and M. Nussbaum (eds.), *Language and Logos* (Cambridge, 1982), 95–114.

Barney, R. *A Reading of Plato's Cratylus*. Unpublished Ph.D. dissertation. Princeton University, 1996.

———. "Plato on Conventionalism." *Phronêsis* 42 (1997), 143–62.

Baxter, T. M. S. *The Cratylus: Plato's Critique of Naming* (Leiden, 1992).

Bestor, T. W. "Plato's Semantics and Plato's *Cratylus*." *Phronesis* 25 (1980), 306–30.

Brumbaugh, R. "Plato's *Cratylus*: the Order of the Etymologies." *Review of Metaphysics* 11 (1957/8), 502–10.

Calvert, B. "Forms and Flux in Plato's *Cratylus*." *Phronesis* 15 (1970), 26–34.

Chen, L. C. H. "Onomatopeia in the *Cratylus*." *Apeiron* 16 (1982), 86–101.

Demand, N. "The Nomothetes of the *Cratylus*." *Phronesis* 20 (1975), 106–09.

Denyer, N. *Language, Thought, and Falsehood in Ancient Greek Philosophy* (London, 1991). Chapter 5 is on the *Cratylus*.

De Vries, G. J. "Notes on Some Passages of the *Cratylus*." *Mnemosyne* 4 (1955), 290–97.

Fine, G. "Plato on Naming." *Philosophical Quarterly* 27 (1977), 289–301.

Gold, J. "The Ambiguity of 'Name' in Plato's *Cratylus*." *Philosophical Studies* 34 (1978), 223–51.

Gosling, J. C. B. *Plato* (London, 1973).

Gould, J. B. "Plato: About Language: The *Cratylus* Reconsidered." *Apeiron* 3 (1969), 19–31.

Grote, G. *Plato and the Other Companions of Socrates*. 3 vols. (London, 1865). Chapter XXIX is on the *Cratylus*.

Kahn, C. "Language and Ontology in the *Cratylus*." In E. N. Lee *et al.* (eds.), *Exegesis and Argument* (Assen, 1973), 152–76.

Ketchum, R. "Names, Forms, and Conventionalism: *Cratylus* 383–395." *Phronesis* 24 (1979), 133–47.

Kirk, G. S. "The Problem of Cratylus." *American Journal of Philology* 72 (1951), 225–53.

Kretzmann, N. "Plato on the Correctness of Names." *American Philosophical Quarterly* 8 (1971), 126–38.

Levin, S. "What's in a Name? A Reconsideration of the *Cratylus*' Historical Sources and Topics." *Ancient Philosophy* 15 (1995), 91–115.

Loraux, N. "Cratyle à l'Épreuve de Stasis." *Revue de Philosophie Ancienne* 5 (1987), 49–69.

Lorenz, K. and Mittelstrass, J. "On Rational Philosophy of Language: The Programme in Plato's *Cratylus* Reconsidered." *Mind* 76 (1967), 1–20.

Luce, J. V. "The Date of the *Cratylus*." *American Journal of Philology* 85 (1964), 136–54.

———. "The Theory of Ideas in the *Cratylus*." *Phronesis* 10 (1965), 21–36.

————. "Plato on the Truth and Falsity of Names." *Classical Quarterly* 19 (1969), 222–32.

Mackenzie, M. M. A. "Putting the *Cratylus* in Its Place." *Classical Quarterly* 36/1 (1986), 124–50.

Pfeiffer, W. M. True and False Speech in Plato's *Cratylus.*" *Canadian Journal of Philosophy* 2 (1972–3), 87–104.

Reed, N. H. "Plato on Flux, Perception, and Language." *Proceedings of the Cambridge Philological Society* N. S. 18 (1972), 65–77.

Richardson, M. "True and False Names in the *Cratylus.*" *Phronesis* 21 (1976), 135–45.

Robinson, R. "A Criticism of Plato's *Cratylus.*" In his *Essays in Greek Philosophy* (Oxford, 1969).

Rosenstock, B. "Fathers and Sons, Irony in the *Cratylus.*" *Arethusa* 25 (1992), 385–417.

Schofield, M. "A Displacement in the Text of the *Cratylus.*" *Classical Quarterly* 22 (1972), 246–53.

————. "The Dénouement of the *Cratylus.*" In M. Schofield and M. Nussbaum (eds.), *Language and Logos* (Cambridge, 1982), 61–81.

Sedley, D. "The Etymologies in Plato's *Cratylus.*" Forthcoming in *Journal of Hellenic Studies* (1999).

Silverman, A. "Plato's *Cratylus*: The Naming of Nature and the Nature of Naming." *Oxford Studies in Ancient Philosophy* 10 (1992), 25–71.

Spellman, L. "Naming and Knowing: The *Cratylus* on Images." *History of Philosophy Quarterly* 10 (1993), 197–210.

Weingartner, R. H. *The Unity of the Platonic Dialogue: The Cratylus, the Protagoras, the Parmenides* (Indianapolis, 1973).

White, F. C. "On Essences in the *Cratylus.*" *The Southern Journal of Philosophy* 16 (1978), 259–74.

White, N. *Plato on Knowledge and Reality* (Indianapolis, 1976). Chapter VI is on the *Cratylus.*

Williams, B. "Cratylus' Theory of Names and Its Refutation." In M. Schofield and M. Nussbaum (eds.), *Language and Logos* (Cambridge, 1982), 83–93.

INDEX OF NAMES DISCUSSED IN THE *CRATYLUS*

C.D.C. REEVE is Professor of Philosophy and Humanities at Reed College. He is author of *Philosopher-Kings* (Princeton, 1988), *Socrates in the Apology* (Hackett, 1989), and *Practices of Reason* (Oxford, 1992). Hackett published his highly acclaimed revision of the Grube translation of Plato's *Republic* in 1993, and his translation of Aristotle's *Politics* in 1998.